RAISING

AWESOME

KIDS

IN TROUBLED TIMES

RAISING

AWESOME

Sam & Geri Laing

KIDS

IN TROUBLED TIMES

DPI

DISCIPLESHIP
PUBLICATIONS
INTERNATIONAL

One Merrill Street
Woburn, MA 01801
1-800-727-8273
Fax (617) 937-3889

Raising Awesome Kids in Troubled Times
©1994 by Discipleship Publications International
One Merrill Street, Woburn, MA 01801

Cover design: Nora Robbins
Interior design: Scott Vigneault

Third printing, November 1994

ISBN 1-884553-23-0

Dedication

To John Oliver Laing, Sr., and Agnes Laing
and to Frank A. Guba and Jane Guba,

our beloved parents,

*for all of your untold sacrifices,
for all you have given,
we give you our thanks and
our undying love.*

Contents

Acknowledgments

"Writing a book is an adventure: to begin with it is a toy and an amusement, and then it becomes a mistress, and then it becomes a tyrant, and the last phase is that just as you are about to be reconciled to your servitude, you kill the monster and fling him out to the public."

Winston Churchill

Writing this book has certainly ranged from an adventure to one of the most challenging projects we have ever undertaken. We could not have accomplished it without the help, encouragement and prayers of many people, all of whom cannot be listed here.

Carvel Baus organized our typing team and carried much of the load himself, at the cost of many late nights and great personal sacrifice. Kim Mantooth and Joel Hughes spent many hours in typing our manuscript, with smiles on their faces and encouraging words on their lips. To the rest of our team, listed below, our heartfelt thanks: Bill Dearmey (thanks for the all-nighter!), Tracy MacLachlan, John Payne and Buena Wheless. There were many others who are not listed here who also donated their assistance in typing the manuscript. Without their efforts, our task would have been much more difficult.

Elwood Peters and Chris Tilley served as our proofreaders. Their vigilance and expertise were invaluable.

Carol Fiks provided many wonderful ideas from her personal experiences that helped us with our chapter discussing single parents and composite families. Our readings of many other authors are felt throughout this volume, especially those of Dr. James Dobson in the chapter on nurturing confidence in children.

All of the great people at our publishers have been a joy with whom to work and have added to the quality and professionalism of our work immensely. Our gratitude and appreciation are especially extended to Tom and Sheila Jones for their hard work and helpful suggestions.

To Roger Lamb: Your relentless encouragment for us to launch out and do something like this will never be forgotten. To Bill and Laura Boyles: Your support of Sam's academic and literary aspirations have now borne fruit after all these years! To Mitch and Jan Mitchell: Your countless acts of service to us and our family enabled us to take the time to do this; your superb leadership of the Triangle church during those weeks carried the ministry forward to victory. To the rest of the staff at Triangle: your hard work and faithfulness have given us the freedom to write. To all of the members at Triangle church: Your prayers, patience and words of encouragement have carried us all the way to the finish.

To our children: Thank you for letting us tell all the stories about you; thank you for your patience while Mom and Dad were so busy writing this book.

Above all, we thank God for his grace and for giving us a family life we can share with all of you.

Foreword

Praise be to the God and Father of our Lord Jesus Christ, who has blessed us in the heavenly realms with *every* spiritual blessing in Christ (Ephesians 1:3, italics added).

No one scripture more accurately describes my life than this one! God has given me so many incredible gifts that I could never name them all! I have salvation and a perpetually clean slate before God, a close, spiritual family, numerous "best friends" scattered across the country, and an overall fun, fulfilling life! I realize with absolute clarity that every one of these blessings can be attributed solely to the fact that I have Christian parents.

This year more than ever I have come to understand just how crucial it is for teens to know God. Only four months ago, three students from my school committed suicide within two weeks of one another. I felt as if God himself was sending me a wake-up call. For years, I had naively entertained the belief that teens are not *too* bad off spiritually and that most of them will not even think about or comprehend spiritual subjects for a few more years. I could not have been further from the truth.

Since that time, I have spoken with several other students who are desperately seeking answers to their questions about themselves, the purpose of their lives and even about God. Most of their parents have no clue that their children care about such things and probably have very few satisfying answers to give them anyway!

God has finally convinced me that just as much as I do, my friends at school urgently need the guidance of parents who are disciples—not just *good* parents or even *great* parents but disciple parents. All the students who committed suicide came from well-to-do families that appeared to have it all together. However, for all the love, material things, and even worldly wisdom they provided their children, they could not give them the purpose and ultimate peace they so desperately desired.

My purpose in writing about these depressing events is not to discourage readers or condemn the world; rather, I want parents to realize that raising children to know and love God is of utmost importance, and that it can be done! I have been amazed at the incredible ways in which God has blessed my life and other teens' lives through our parents. I wholeheartedly believe that all disciples (not just the leaders) can successfully inspire in their children the desire for an eternal relationship with God and can even have close relationships with their teenagers themselves! Believe me, my parents have spent innumerable hours of laborious Bible study and many nights of tearful prayer—most of which took place on account of me—in order to get our family to where it needed to be (of course, every one of these spiritual battles occurred many, many years ago, and I have been an angel ever since!). Although building a godly, happy family does take intense effort, "with God all things are possible" (Matthew 19:26).

Of all that my parents have done for me, the things I most appreciate always will be their unashamed effort to put God first in our family, their firm discipline, their complete, ungrudging forgiveness, and their compassion and understanding. It is my prayer that, if you glean nothing else from this book, you will grow in these areas and so build families that truly ". . .shine before men, that they may see your good deeds and praise your Father in heaven" (Matthew 5:14).

Elizabeth Laing
Age 17
March 1994

11

Introduction

"I'm out here, Daddy. . .I'm out here, Daddy. . .I'm out here, Daddy. . ." My daughter, repeating her words in a rhythmic monotone as only a two year old can, seemed to go on and on, insistent but polite in her determination to be heard. She stood in the kitchen and spoke through the closed door into the dining room where I was seated at the table working. It was Saturday night, and the hour was drawing late. I still had no idea for the sermon I was to preach the next morning. Anxiety and frustration mounted within me, only further stifling the ability to think perceptively and creatively. The voice of young Elizabeth, who had just had her bath and was all set for bed, only made matters worse. She just wanted to say good night, but I was preoccupied.

"Not now, honey, Daddy's busy."

But she would not be turned away.

"I'm out here, Daddy," came back the reply.

I repeated my rebuff a few more times, as pleasantly as I could, but to no avail.

"I'm out here, Daddy... I'm out here, Daddy"

I tried the silent treatment. Maybe if I did not say anything, she would get tired and go away.

But after a few moments, the little voice spoke again, "I'm out here, Daddy."

I finally realized this was getting nowhere and that I would have to let her in.

"Okay, honey, come on in, but Daddy is really busy."

The self-closing swinging door that separated the dining room from the kitchen creaked slowly open, then closed with the *ka whoom-whoom-whoom* sound it always made as it settled back into its normal position. I kept my eyes glued to my work, hoping that Elizabeth would now be satisfied. She silently entered and stood a few feet behind my chair. I continued to work, straining for a sermon topic, but nothing would come to mind. My concentration was so intense that I completely forgot that my young daughter was still in the room. Then I heard, from directly behind my chair, the soft, small voice of Elizabeth saying, "I'm in here, Daddy."

I'm in here, Daddy. Isn't that what our children are trying to tell us? They are "in here" with us, and they need us. The world is "out there," and it is troubling and hard, and seemingly getting more difficult to cope with every passing year. We simply **must** take the few precious years we have with our children and make the most of the time.

This is a book to help you to be a better parent. In it, Geri and I share with you some of what we have gleaned from the Scriptures and what we have learned from the wonderful experience of raising our four children. We hope these lessons will help you as much as they have helped us.

We do not presume to be perfect parents or to have a perfect family. But we are trying to do it God's way, and he has blessed us amazingly. We love the life God has given us, and our family is having a blast living it together!

Let me assure you that our children have given us their permission to tell you all the different stories that involve them. We do not wish to embarrass our kids, nor do we long for them to be put on a pedestal. They, like their mom and dad, are only human, with their strengths and weaknesses. If sharing some of the specifics about our household and its members can help you, then the Laing family is happy for you to know us as we really are.

Please, study this book carefully before you try to implement everything in it. More than a "how to" manual, it is intended to be a means to help you think and act with godly attitudes. So many things we discuss in these pages are difficult to present with the proper weight, emphasis and clarity and can be easily misunderstood and misapplied. We especially want you to grasp that the strong discipline and high standards that we urge in child rearing must be carried out in an atmosphere of love, joy and happiness.

If you and your family need additional help and advice, we encourage you to seek the counsel of mature, spiritual disciples and experienced church leaders. The situations some of you face may require wise, objective help, perhaps over a period of time.

But we never finished our story! Elizabeth was left standing forlornly behind my chair, wasn't she?

After hearing her words, I put down my pen, turned to her, smiled and took her into my arms. Warm tears of affection welled up freely in my eyes. I held her and talked with her for a few minutes, hugged her again and put her down. She toddled back to her room smiling and contented, ready to be put to bed.

I do not remember what I preached the next morning, and I'm sure no one else does either. But as long as I live, I will never forget the lesson God taught me that Saturday night so many years ago.

My daughter was trying to tell me something, and at first, I was not listening. She needed my love and attention and did not know how to say it. She wanted to be with me, but I was "too busy." Sometimes, even today, as a young woman of 17, Elizabeth still comes quietly into the room where I am and just sits down. After a few moments of silence I ask, "Honey, would you like to talk for a minute?" and we do. We always hug at the end, and she always walks away contented and smiling. As I watch her leave, I am thankful I finally got the message that night when she was only two years old.

May you hear the voices of your children, whether they speak aloud or reach out to you silently with longing in their eyes. They are with you for only a few precious years. Sooner than you realize, they will be "out there" in a world that can devour them if you have not raised them well. Give them all you can while they are "in here" with you in your home. They will turn out awesome!

And if we, by the efforts we have made in this volume, can help you to do a better job of that, then we have not written in vain.

Sam and Geri Laing
Cary, North Carolina
March 1994

FOUNDATIONS

1

First Things First

Unless the Lord builds the house, its builders labor in vain (Psalm 127:1).

MOST OF US HAVE SOMEONE, OR SOMETHING, THAT WE LOVE most in this world. Who or what is it for you? Think now, and be honest. If you need help, ask your children to answer the question for you. If they are old enough, they will know, and they will tell you the unadorned truth. Upon the answer to this question hinge all of your hopes, your dreams and your capacities to raise your children to a joyful end. If the answer is what it should be, then the rest of this book can be a powerful tool to help you. But if the answer is wrong, then you are doomed to frustration, heartache and failure. No amount of counsel, however wise, can repair your house, if the Lord is not the builder.

Jesus must be our first love. He must be our life's greatest passion. He must *be* our life, not just a part of it. He will not be added in as one more calendar item to "round out" our personal or family life. He must be the hub of the wheel, not one of many spokes. He will not be the copilot. He is either the pilot, or he is out of the plane.

Jesus expected people to be disciples:

> And anyone who does not carry his cross and follow me cannot be my disciple (Luke 14:27).

He elaborated with these words:

> ..."If anyone would come after me, he must deny himself and take up his cross and follow me. For whoever wants to save his life will lose it, but whoever loses his life for me and for the gospel will save it. What good is it for a man to gain the whole world, yet forfeit his soul?" (Mark 8:34-36).

Paul said it this way:

> When Christ, who is your life, appears, then you also will appear with him in glory (Colossians 3:4).

> I have been crucified with Christ and I no longer live, but Christ lives in me... (Galatians 2:20).

> For to me, to live is Christ, and to die is gain (Philippians 1:21).

We must put first things first. This is the key to everything, not just the impractical theory we discard before getting to the "real thing" of how to raise kids.

Why is it that some church-going people find their marriages empty and in shambles and their children increasingly disinterested in spiritual things? It is because merely being religious will not do the job. Even deep involvement in a fired-up church is not enough. Your kids must see that Jesus is a real person to you and that you walk with him and love him as a brother. Your faith must make a real difference in the person you are at home, because that is who you really are. You can't fake it there. There is no acting at home, just real life. Kids can spot a fake, a sham, or external devotion a mile away, and they will be turned off and even embittered by anything they perceive as less than genuine.

When asked what was the greatest commandment in the Law—that one thing which God valued most highly—Jesus announced that it was to "love the Lord your God with all your heart and with all your soul and with all your mind and with all your strength" (Mark 12:30). We are not committed to commitment or disciples of discipleship; we are committed to *God* and disciples of a *person*, of Jesus Christ himself. That is the difference between someone who is religious and someone who deeply loves God. It is also the difference between those who can reach their children for Christ and those who cannot.

Such a life is attractive. It is winsome. It is above the grind, it is fun, it is awesome, and it is glorious! Your children will look at you and marvel. They will admire you. They will want to be like you. They will see that although Jesus calls for commitment, his yoke is easy and his burden is light. They will sense your deep inner spring of spiritual life and long to drink of it themselves. They will say in their hearts, "My dad and my mom have something inside that is *real*. It gives them love, joy, and peace that I see nowhere else. My friends and their parents outside God's kingdom don't have it. My unbelieving teachers don't have it. All the loose-living superstars in the world don't have what my parents have. I *must* be what my parents are so I can have what they have."

I want to share with you a birthday card my son Jonathan wrote for me when he was 10 years old. I do this to let you see how highly a child values our love for God, and how keenly they can perceive it, even from an early age.

10/7/98

Dear Dad,

Happy B day!!!!!!!!!!!! You made it! Ha! Ha! Ha! Ha!!! I love you so very much!!!!! My arm would fall off if I tryed list all the things you do for me! You are the best dad, on this Earth!! You are so discipline, you have quiet-times every day, but most of all you have such an awesome heart for God!!! I really admire that alot. You have taught me so much! Like football, I use to not even be able to throw one! With-out you I would be a wimpy little kid!! 😊 I hope you've had an awesome birthday and like your new things!! I love you alot! Goodnight!!!!!!!!!!!

Love,
Jonathan Laing
JONATHAN LAING

There are many things in Jonathan's card that touched me, but that which moved and surprised me the most were his feelings about my closeness to God. Jonathan sees that and wants it for himself. The battle for his soul is more than half won already!

Some of you have never made your decision to be a disciple of Jesus. You need to find someone to teach you the Bible and help you make your commitment. Your own soul and the souls of your loved ones depend upon it.

Others of us made that decision in the past, but where are we today? We were at one time zealous and devoted—probably *before* we got married or had children. What happened? Various life changes have distracted us—have we lost our first love for Christ? As my wife Geri often says, "The longer I live, the more I see how hard it is to make it all the way, faithful to the end."

It is so easy to allow "life's worries, riches and pleasures" and "the deceitfulness of wealth, and the desires for other things" to come in and choke out our relationship with God (Luke 8:14, Mark 4:19). The gifts God has given us—our spouses, our children, our jobs—can become paramount and displace our love for the Giver. Or, we can allow even legitimate concerns to so worry and distract us that our minds are no longer spiritually focused.

If this is your condition, seek the Lord again with all your heart. Put him back in the place of supremacy. If God is first, you have the foundation upon which to build an awesome family.

❧

Assuming God is first, who's next on our list? Who gets the nod for second place? Let me say it plainly: *Next in line to God comes our husband or wife.* They must be that special person, the one we love more than anyone else on earth. More than our love for our mother or father, more than our love for our children, or anyone or anything else, our devotion to our lifetime companion must be the greatest earthly love of all.

23

Our spouse is the one person to whom we are physically and spiritually united until death. Listen to the words of Jesus:

> "Haven't you read," he replied, "that at the beginning the Creator 'made them male and female,' and said 'For this reason a man will leave his father and mother and be united to his wife, and the two, will become one flesh'? So they are no longer two but one. Therefore what God has joined together, let man not separate" (Matthew 19:4-6).

One day (hopefully!) our offspring will grow up and leave home. We raise our children to go out and build their own lives, but we stay with our marriage partner for *life*. The kids are our flesh and blood, but we are *one flesh* with our spouse. The difference is absolutely critical.

Some of us, to make up for the affection we lack from or for our spouse, have poured all our love into our children. This is foolish and selfish. It ultimately damages the kids. They are not meant to be in that special position. That place is reserved for the husband or wife *alone*. If your world revolves around your children, it makes them arrogant, insecure or both. Kids do not find their true joy and confidence from being put on a pedestal; they find it first from God, then from their mom and dad being deeply in love.

It is so easy for a marriage to grow cold, to gradually lose "that lovin' feeling," for the exciting, romantic love to fade away. We find ourselves saying things like, "Well, we're so busy, and we have kids now, and we just don't have time for each other anymore, and we don't really talk like we used to." Come on, bag the excuses! Do something before you lose the chance!

Take an honest look at your marriage. Is there bickering and arguing? A tense, cold atmosphere? A war for supremacy? Cutting, sarcastic, harsh remarks? Raised voices? Arguments in front of or within earshot of the kids? I appeal to you, for your sake, for the Lord's sake, for your children's sake, take radical action and get help!

Sometimes, we think the children can't tell when we aren't getting along well, or we think that our problems have little effect on them. Let's not kid ourselves! Those little eyes and ears are fine-tuned to our frequency. They can sense when things aren't right between Mom and Dad, and it troubles them. Kids hate it when their parents bicker and quarrel. They long so desperately for us to love each other, to laugh together and to be close.

Why is it that when Mom and Dad hug, the kids want to nuzzle in between, and start giggling and teasing? It is because they *love* it when we love each other. It gives them a sense of peace, happiness, and security and lets them know that all is well and that the family is going to stay together.

Much of the anger and rebellion in kids today can be traced back to problem marriages. Children living in fear and tension cannot relax and enjoy life. They worry their little hearts out. They try to fix everything. They choose sides. They end up resenting their parents, disliking themselves and possibly even blaming themselves.

People often ask Geri and me why our children seem secure, confident and joyful. They observe that they respect each other, relate to people well, are highly motivated and are comfortable with authority. I offer that it is because they have a perfect father, but I don't get many takers!

The secret, besides our relationship with God, is our relationship with each other. Geri and I really love and like each other. We get along well and resolve any disagreements on the very day they occur. We are comfortable in our roles (see Chapters 2 and 3) and have a good romantic life. We certainly make no pretensions of perfection (for us or our children), but we have a good marriage. We have made it so by hard work, prayer, lots of apologies and by submitting ourselves to God. Such a union is the good soil in which our children have grown.

I'll never forget the incident that so clearly showed me this lesson. It happened when our son David was about three. We were in the car, and David and a playmate were in the back seat. Geri and I leaned over and gave each other a little kiss. David's pal immediately yelled out, "Oooooooo! Your mom and dad *kissed!* My mom and dad *never* kiss!" From his tone, you would have thought we had been caught shoplifting or something. David looked at his friend quizzically. Then he turned to him, leaned over, and said proudly: "Well, my mom and dad kiss *a lot* !"

I've got it all figured out now, and here it is: To love God first, and to deeply and happily love one another, is the greatest gift parents can ever give their children. If we have this going for us, *we can do it* ! We can raise "Awesome Kids in Troubled Times!"

CHAPTER 2

Husband and Father

Husbands, love your wives, just as Christ loved the church
and gave himself up for her...Fathers, do not exasperate
your children; instead, bring them up in the training and
instruction of the Lord (Ephesians 5:25, 6:4).

MY LAST MEMORY OF MY FATHER FOREVER WILL BE WITH ME. HE
was lying upon his bed in our home, emaciated by
cancer, knowing the end was near. I was 12 years old,
the youngest of five children. He called us all in, spoke his
last words, and we saw him for the final time. I do not remember
what he said. I only remember the love I felt and the gift he gave
me. He wanted me to have his beautiful 20-gauge shotgun, the one
he used for quail hunting. I remember the embrace, the tears and
his heart for me. I treasure the gift he gave me and the memories
it evokes of the wonderful times we spent together hunting in the
North Florida fields where I grew up.

I have thought back through my childhood many times. I
have sought to recall every positive, joyful memory of my dad and

our relationship. There are many, and they move me to tears even as I write these words.

The sad thing is that my dad and I did not connect that deeply during those brief 12 years we had together. It wasn't that he did not try or that he did not care; some things just got in the way. My father had a temper and would sometimes raise his voice, not necessarily at me, but perhaps at someone else or at something that frustrated him. Now that I am older and I have to confront my own temper, I have much more understanding and compassion for him. But at the time, as a child, I withdrew in fear, hurt, rebellion and anger.

It was years later, after viewing the film *Field of Dreams*, that I saw my problem. The movie told the story of a rebellious son's vision of his dad when his father was still a young man, "before life had broken him down." It moved me so deeply (as it did many men) that afterwards I could scarcely speak. It sparked in me a deeper love for my father and enabled me to face and excise the root of bitterness that had so long grown within my heart. The burden of years of hurt and alienation disappeared, leaving behind only the wish that I, too, could have another chance to see my dad and to be as close to him as we both had longed.

I have since vowed that whatever I did, I would be close to my children. I promised God with all my heart to express to them my love, to be approachable, and to never allow any of them to be distant from me. God has blessed that commitment in a wonderful way. One of the incomparable rewards of my life is the closeness I enjoy with all four of my children, and I know they all feel the same way.

Our relationship with our father is, in many ways, the defining relationship in all of our lives. From it we develop our fundamental view of God and of ourselves. From this most basic of bonds also comes our response to authority and our self-confidence. This is why God places the responsibility of training children squarely upon the father: "Fathers...bring them up in the training and instruction of the Lord" (Ephesians 6:4). This is not to diminish the mother's responsibility, but to give the proper emphasis to the father's role, a role so grievously neglected and misconceived in today's world. I believe that the increasing violence, chaos and emotional disturbance in many teenagers is a direct result of the absent or failing fathers in our homes. Paul described the responsibilities of a husband and father in Ephesians 5:22-6:4, one of the definitive passages on the subject. His instructions can be summarized by two things: to *lead* and to *love*. We will examine them both.

Part 1

The Father as Leader

"For the husband is the head of the wife as Christ is the head of the church" (Ephesians 5:23) and as such is the head of the entire family. This means that you, as a father, are in charge. Under God, this responsibility is yours. It is neither arrogant nor presumptuous for you to lead. It is wrong not to lead. The marriage is a partnership, to be sure, but the husband is the senior partner. The family functions as a group, but it is not a democracy. It has a leader who will listen, weigh and consider, but who has the charge, challenge and accountability for the final decision.

Men and women are of equal worth in the eyes of God (Galatians 3:26-28), but in marriage and in the home they have different roles:

> Wives, submit to your husbands as to the Lord. For the husband is the head of the wife as Christ is the head of the church, his body, of which he is the Savior. Now as the church submits to Christ, so also wives should submit to their husbands in everything (Ephesians 5:22-24).

That men are to lead is not merely social convention. It is intrinsic to the very nature of creation:

> Now I want you to realize that the head of every man is
> Christ, and the head of the woman is man, and the head of
> Christ is God (1 Corinthians 11:3).

Whatever the full meaning of these passages may be, they make it clear that men are equipped and charged by God with the responsibility of leadership in the home.

As with all else in the Scriptures, we hurt ourselves and those close to us when we ignore or distort God's plan. Untold harm comes to families, to children, and indeed to whole cultures and nations when homes are not built on the principle of husband/father leadership. Even in the church, we have been far too influenced by worldly and unbiblical thinking on this point. We will live to pay a price dearer than we can imagine unless we restore the role of male leadership in marriage and the family according to God's plan.

The place to start is in your own home. We will examine four different aspects of the father as leader.

1. Strength and Conviction

> "...then choose for yourselves this day whom you will
> serve...But as for me and my household, we will serve the
> Lord" (Joshua 24:15).

Fathers, we should be the Rock of our family who, with Joshua of old, says "my family will serve the Lord." We should be the one to hold high the standard of absolute commitment to Jesus, the church and righteous living. When the call goes forth in the kingdom of God for response and sacrifice, we must lead the way. Our personal walk with God and our zeal for saving the lost should be an inspiration. We must strive mightily to be the strongest and most spiritual disciple in the entire family.

The responsibility to initiate, plan and conduct family devotionals rests on our shoulders. It is also our job to make sure that the children are being discipled to Christ. We should also pray with and teach our wives and urge them forward in their walk with God.

If we have convictions, our family will have them. If we are strong, our household will be. As we lead, they follow. It is a natural thing for children to want to follow the lead of their father. They do it instinctively. But this is also true of a negative example. How many times have we seen the children of spiritually apathetic and indifferent fathers follow suit? Even if Mother or Grandmother is a saint, it is usually not enough to turn the tide of a father's bad influence. As soon as they are old enough to go their own way, these kids quit the church. Boys, especially, will conclude that church is well and good for weaklings, for little kids, or for old people, but not for them.

Men, we must not buy into the world's idea that being spiritual is a "woman thing." No! Look at the men of the Bible like Moses, Joshua, David, John the Baptist, Peter, Paul and Jesus. They were *men* in every sense of the word—in their masculinity, strength of character and courage. These are our true models of manhood.

As head of his family, the church, Jesus is strong. And we should be, too. As head of our families, it is requisite that we be strong emotionally. The challenges of life must not break us down into depression and despair. If we fall, who will stand? It is a sad thing to see the wife or children trying to be the emotional glue of the family because the father has been rendered an angry, introverted, indecisive, self-pitying basket case by difficulties and pressures. Life is hard. Strength is needed, not only for Christ's sake, but also for our families' sake. " For God did not give us a spirit of timidity, but a spirit of power, of love and of self-discipline" (2 Timothy 1:7).

31

It is needful to be strong *physically*. Yes, you heard me right. A man should not be soft and effeminate. We do not have to be Mr. Olympia contenders, but we should not be foppish embarrassments to our gender. Peter describes the wife as "the weaker partner" (1 Peter 3:7), but I must say that some of us have made the "Big Fisherman" a liar! We are weaker than our wives spiritually, emotionally and physically! No wonder we get no respect!

Get out, and get some exercise. Take off some fat; put on some beef. Tone up your flaccid, flabby physique. Detach yourself from the couch. Get moving. Play some sports. Break a sweat, for crying out loud!

Jesus was a carpenter. He walked everywhere he went. Be like him. Your wife will admire you and be attracted to you. Your daughters will be proud for their girlfriends (and boyfriends!) to meet you. Your sons will love to spend time with you. There is something impressive about a man who retains a youthful energy and power as the years advance. What a difference it makes in your leadership! [1]

An incident that brought this issue home to me happened back in the late '70s when my daughter Elizabeth was three years old. There was a popular TV show about a wimpy guy who, upon provocation, transformed into a huge, unbelievably muscular, green behemoth called "The Incredible Hulk." While watching the show one night, Elizabeth turned to me and said, "Daddy, I love the Incredible Hulk. He's big like *you* are!" Ever since that time, I knew that this wonderful child was destined for greatness. I also knew I'd better get in shape and stay in shape!

---

[1] Certainly those of you who face various physical challenges and limitations should not feel robbed of your manhood or that you can't show your children a masculine example. You may not be able to do what others can do, but if you face whatever difficulty you have with courage, determination and faith, you will win the hearts and respect of your children. As Paul said in another context: "The gift is acceptable according to what one has, not according to what one does not have" (2 Corinthians 8:12). Whatever situation you are in, give your best. Do that and God will bless you and your children.

2. Provision and Protection

> If anyone does not provide for his relatives, and especially for his immediate family, he has denied the faith and is worse than an unbeliever (1 Timothy 5:8).

So Paul, tell us, how do you really feel about deadbeat dads? Don't hold back, now!

Our families should never have to worry about where the next meal is coming from, if the lights and phone are going to be turned off, if the car is going to be repossessed, or if there will be a roof over their heads or clothes to wear. I simply do not want my wife and kids ever to be haunted by that kind of insecurity. They can know that as long as Dad is there, they have absolutely nothing to worry about. To me, it is an issue not only of my commitment to God, but of my manhood. If my Heavenly Father provides for all my physical needs (Matthew 6:25-34), should I not imitate him in caring for my children?

Stop living off your parents, the church, your friends and the government. Stop making your wife carry the financial load, working herself to death to keep the family from going under. Be a man. Get a job—one that pays a real salary and provides some benefits. Some men are dreamers and never "settle down and earn the bread they eat" (2 Thessalonians 3:12). Heed the wise words of Solomon: "He who works his land will have abundant food, but the one who chases fantasies will have his fill of poverty" (Proverbs 28:19).

You say you can't find a job? I don't think so. Find something, work hard at it, and you will ultimately advance. Go to school and learn a skill. "Do you see a man skilled in his work? He will serve before kings; he will not serve before obscure men" (Proverbs 22:29).

Get adequate medical insurance. Make arrangements that if you should die or be incapacitated, your family will not become dependent. Be on top of your finances so that there is adequate cash flow and timely payment of bills. Start a savings account to provide a cash reserve for emergencies and larger purchases, and start planning now for your children's college education.

Take care of things around the house. If there is a yard, mow it. If there are leaves, rake them. If there is snow, shovel it. If there is furniture to be moved, get up off it and move it! Do the repair jobs and maintenance work. Change the filters, look after the car, paint the walls, take out the garbage. There are many frustrated wives out there who seemingly cannot get their husbands to lift a finger to help them. The kids will see this and will either disrespect us for our indolence or cheerfully imitate us in it. Happy is the family with a hard-working father! "If a man is lazy, the rafters sag; if his hands are idle, the house leaks" (Ecclesiastes 10:18).

But fathers are more than providers—we are also protectors. As protector we look out for and guard our families physically, emotionally and spiritually. We should watch out for our wives and children, making sure they are physically safe. There is no place for fretting and worry, but for calm, careful vigilance. If any family member is in a situation where they will be beaten down, crushed or completely overwhelmed, then it is time to act. We cannot and should not shield them from the realities of life, but we must protect them from any forces before which they are helpless.

3. Training and Teaching

> Fathers... bring them up in the training and instruction of the Lord (Ephesians 6:4).

We will devote a great deal of time (Chapter 6) to the spiritual training of children. Here I speak of our role as a coach and a mentor—teaching kids the nuts-and-bolts skills of life. As fathers, we teach and train nonstop. With younger children, it may be teaching a simple physical activity such as eating or tying shoes;

with pre-teens and teens, it could be training in manners or in dating etiquette.

Some of us dads need to get out and work with our kids, especially our sons, on athletics. We need to teach them how to throw and catch, how to hit a baseball, and how to kick a soccer ball. Do not underestimate the importance of this kind of teaching! It gives our kids confidence and makes life more fun when they don't feel like klutzes on the playground. I have spent lots of time, especially with my sons, teaching them basic sports skills. They love me for it, and it's fun for me, too. They perform at an above-average level simply because I taught them some fundamentals.

But what if you never had anyone who gave you this kind of training and you feel a bit inadequate at trying to help your kids out? Don't despair. It's not too late to learn a few things. Get some other guys to teach you. Don't be too prideful to ask. Get them together with you and your child. The worst mistake you can make is to do nothing. Certainly worth is not tied to excelling in sports, but kids who learn some basics won't go through life feeling like clumsy outcasts.

Children love to learn, to feel that they are being taken somewhere in skills and knowledge. Therefore, always teach. From how to drive a car to how to respond to teasing, equip them to handle life. Why else does God let us keep them for almost 20 years, if not to train them in what they need to know?

4. Model of Masculinity

> So God created man in his own image, in the image of God he created him; male and female he created them (Genesis 1:27).

God made us either male or female, and kids are extremely aware of the difference! One of the great issues in growing up is dealing with "who you are" as a boy or as a girl. From a very early age, children are busy trying to figure all of this out.

The world is so mixed up on this, it is absolutely scary. We have men wanting to be women and women wanting to be men. The superstars openly flaunt their sexual aberrations. Androgyny is the thing. You can't tell who is who or what is what without a program! The women's movement cries one thing, the gays and lesbians another; and even in our schools there is a burgeoning clamor to present homosexuality, lesbianism and cohabitation as acceptable "lifestyles."

> Therefore God gave them over in the sinful desires of their hearts to sexual impurity for the degrading of their bodies with one another. They exchanged the truth of God for a lie, and worshiped and served created things rather than the Creator—who is forever praised. Amen. Because of this, God gave them over to shameful lusts. Even their women exchanged natural relations for unnatural ones. In the same way the men also abandoned natural relations with women and were inflamed with lust for one another. Men committed indecent acts with other men, and received in themselves the due penalty for their perversion (Romans 1:24-27).

The challenges and problems in this area can be overwhelming. What can a father do? My answer is this: Read this chapter all the way through and model healthy masculinity. The real thing will outshine the twisted, warped ways of the world. Your kids will see you and know who, and what, a real man is, and what sexuality is all about.

Homosexuality is not natural. No young boy was made that way by God. In my counseling experience, I have found that it is the exploiting of the young, the weak and the naive by predatory older males that creates a homosexual. A great relationship with a strong, affectionate father reduces to virtually zero the chances for a boy to fall into this horrible pit.

What about the son who is shy, withdrawn, or effeminate, one who is a bit of a "mama's boy" or a "sissy"? This special young boy needs to be drawn into a close relationship with his father! Give him plenty of your time. Don't reject him. Don't disdain or ridicule him. Don't pretend these traits aren't there. Instead, put in the good. Teach him to relate confidently to other boys—don't let him hang out with the girls just because it is easier. Teach him sports and manly skills. Don't bully him into a strict macho mold; instead, work with him to have masculine mannerisms. Model away and teach away the soft, lispy voice and girlish giggle. If he is musically or artistically inclined there is nothing wrong with that. Simply encourage a masculine expression of it.

Such a bonding between father and son will have a powerful effect. Your son will gain confidence. He will not feel different or weird, and he will not retreat from the legitimate male world. If he experiences the temptation of homosexual sin, he will have the ability to resist.

Daughters need a strong, affectionate father. It gives them security. They love the sense of approval and love that comes from a special closeness with their dad. If you are kind, strong and close to your daughter, she will want to marry someone like you. She will not seek fulfillment from sexual escapades with boys who want to take advantage of her insecurities. She will not need to say "yes" sexually to prove anything to anyone. And she will one day make someone a wonderful wife!

5. With Liberty and Justice for All

> The boys grew up, and Esau became a skillful hunter, a man of the open country, while Jacob was a quiet man, staying among the tents. Isaac, who had a taste for wild game, loved Esau, but Rebekah loved Jacob (Genesis 25:27-28).

> When his brothers saw that their father loved him more than any of them, they hated him and could not speak a kind word to him (Genesis 37:4).

37

> Acquitting the guilty and condemning the innocent—the
> Lord detests them both (Proverbs 17:15).

As the leader, we fathers must see that there is respect given to all, and we must rule justly in any areas of dispute. Playing favorites is deadly. Look at the years of pain and suffering in the families of Isaac and Jacob brought on by the folly of favoritism.

Who must be respected?

Mother

Sometimes in families with strong fathers, the children do not respect and honor the mother. They look upon her as weak. We can become party to the problem if we engage in any criticism or teasing which degrades our wives. We must spot this and respond swiftly to correct it.

My children know that I respect their mother. If I see them giving her anything less than complete, attentive obedience, I move to her support.

Younger or weaker children

Our two oldest are strong personalities. They are quick with an answer, and they speak out freely. When Jonathan came along, we had to make room for him in conversation. At the dinner table, while he was trying to get his sentences figured out, the conversation had long since moved to other subjects. And when he did try to speak, his older siblings helped him out by finishing his sentences for him! Geri noticed Jonathan's growing frustration and told me about it. I took immediate action. We talked about it in family devotional time and decided to give Jonathan the floor whenever he wanted it—all he had to do was raise his hand. We then had to continually remind his older brother and sister not to interrupt. It worked! So well, in fact, that Jonathan started putting his hand up too much! We then had to teach him not to abuse his privileges.

When Alexandra came along, almost six years younger than the next in line, we had to go through this again. She would not sit, as did Jonathan, and let her frustrations build. Oh, no! She would speak right up in the middle of someone else's sentence, on a completely different subject. Tension was building and feelings were getting hurt. Once again, I had to act to secure everyone's rights.

These may seem to be trivial issues, but they are not. In the life of a child, they are huge. As kids get older, the issues become obviously more critical. But your role as dispenser of justice starts from Day One, and it is one of your most vital roles. (See Chapters 5 and 9 for more discussion on respect and harmony among children.)

Part 2

The Father as Lover

Authority without love creates fear and rebellion. If we want to raise awesome kids, we need to lead *and* love. The combination is powerful and will bond us to our children for life.

1. Compassion and Caring

> The Lord is compassionate and gracious,
>   slow to anger, abounding in love.
> He will not always accuse,
>   nor will he harbor his anger forever;
> he does not treat us as our sins deserve
>   or repay us according to our iniquities.
> For as high as the heavens are above the earth,
>   so great is his love for those who fear him;
>   as far as the east is from the west,
>   so far has he removed our transgressions
>   from us.
> As a father has compassion on his children,

> so the Lord has compassion on those who
> fear him;
> for he knows how we are formed,
> he remembers that we are dust
> (Psalm 103:8-14).

Fatherly Care

God cares! He is aware of our needs, our feelings, our problems, and he is concerned. There is nothing too great or too small to escape his notice or to be beneath or beyond his love.

Fathers, we need to imitate this caring. We must take notice of our children. Are they happy? Sad? Worried? Burdened? We need to watch their eyes, listen to their words, and watch their body language. Our care should flow out as a healthy, refreshing stream. We ought to be a fountainhead of love and concern for our wives and children and always be available to meet the need whatever it is and whenever it arises.

Many of us are oblivious to our children's needs. They are going through struggles with homework, schoolmates and a myriad of other things, and we aren't tuned in! They feel distant from us. We are up there in the clouds, consumed with work or our own problems. They may drop hints or say something in passing that should alert us to a need. Sometimes our wives will see something wrong with the kids and try to tell us, but we aren't listening, and the opportunity passes us by.

The day will come when our children will go to someone else because they have given up trying to reach us. They will have no desire to talk to us anymore. Our hearts will break and we will wonder, "Why can't I reach my kids?" The reason is that we weren't there *when they reached for us.*

Fatherly Compassion

Not only caring for, but feeling with, is the way a father loves. It is a great comfort to know that God hurts for us and with us. He feels what we feel. He is not coldly logical. His great heart goes out to us. "...But while he was still a long way off, his father saw him and was filled with compassion for him; he ran to his son, threw his arms around him and kissed him" (Luke 15:20).

We need to put ourselves in our children's shoes, to remember what it was like to be a kid. Many children's problems are solved simply by them knowing that we feel with them and for them.

Fatherly Forgiveness

When children have done wrong, they need to ask our forgiveness, and we need to grant it. They need to know definitely that they are forgiven and that there is no cloud hanging over their heads. Let them know that it is over and done with. We should not put our children in the doghouse of disapproval, where they feel they never quite have our blessing.

Fatherly Understanding

> ...for he knows how we are formed, he remembers that we are dust (Psalm 103:14).

Our children are...children! They are young, immature, weak, clumsy and foolish. They sneeze, snort, stink, slip, stumble and snicker. We should expect a lot, but we must make wise allowance for immaturity. Let them be kids. The world has enough proper, pompous, sanitized adults to go around. Give them time to grow up. Remember—God is patient with us!

2. Encouragement and Inspiration

> You know that we dealt with each of you as a father deals with his own children, encouraging, comforting, and urging you to live lives worthy of God, who calls you into his kingdom and glory (1 Thessalonians 2:11-12).

Life is hard. It is especially hard for kids. They get plenty of ridicule, teasing and "nyah nyah nyah's" from their peers. It is easy to lose heart. How many kids could do so much more but fail because no one is there to encourage or inspire them?

There is immense power in a father's encouragement. There is a mystical, almost magical energy unleashed when Dad says, "You can do it." If the head guy believes you can, then you can!

Young Timothy was well spoken of by the church (Acts 16:2) but he had weaknesses. He lacked confidence (2 Timothy 1:8, 1 Corinthians 16:10), could lose motivation (2 Timothy 1:6-7), got ill frequently (1 Timothy 5:23), and tended to be lazy (1 Timothy 4:13-15). This young man possessed talent, conviction and heart, but needed someone to believe in him and train him into greatness. Apparently, he had never had a strong male spiritual influence (Acts 16:1, 2 Timothy 1:5).

Paul met Timothy and promptly took him into his heart and under his wing. He became his "father in the faith" (1 Corinthians 4:17). By his encouragement and inspiration he turned this underachieving young man into the dynamic leader of the huge and powerful church in Ephesus. Such is the result of a father's inspiration!

Have great vision for your children. Impart it to them and encourage them unceasingly as they struggle to learn and accomplish. Do not pressure them—inspire them!

One of our jobs as fathers is to wisely and soberly assess our children's gifts and talents and to direct them into an area where they can excel. You need to get them excited and help them to want it from within themselves. Don't let them spin their wheels trying to do something for which they are not suited.

I coached boys' soccer for four years. On my rosters I had everyone from superstars to guys who could barely kick the ball. My job was to believe in and inspire every player and to give each one a sense of his importance to our team. I had to find each player's best position, where his strengths were maximized and his weaknesses were minimized.

There were coaches in our league who just put their boys out in a big mass on the field and let them play. Some coaches "led" by cursing, screaming and berating their players. Others put all their efforts into one or two great athletes, depending on them to carry the team.

My assistants and I coached every player to the maximum of his potential. We accepted them where they were and took them higher. We encouraged each boy as he improved.

They loved it! They had fun! Why? Because each one had a place, felt important, and improved as a player and as a person. In those four years, we won two championships and were in the playoffs the other two times. It was not that we had teams stacked with talent. It was that we got the most out of all 16 players.

My challenge to fathers is this: Be the great inspirer and encourager of your children! Let it be you who thinks they are great and who picks them up when they fall. They will love you for it, and their gratitude and accomplishments will be your reward.

3. Humility and Approachability

> ...All of you, clothe yourselves with humility toward one another, because, "God opposes the proud but gives grace to the humble" (1 Peter 5:5).

Our families know assuredly that we are imperfect; we might as well admit it! A part of our love for them will be our refusal to wear a mask of superiority or to pretend that we are always right. I have found that since I bear the most responsibility in my house, then I make the most mistakes. I have often said, "No one in my house apologizes more than I do." If we are quick to demand apologies but rarely or reluctantly give them, we set up everyone for resentment.

Strong leadership, to some of us, means creating a mystique of infallibility. We feel that to reveal weakness would cause in our followers a loss of confidence and diminution of respect. Far from it! The most powerful and endearing leaders I know are men and women without pretension. Like Paul, they say, "I am the chief of sinners." When they confess their weaknesses and sins, I find myself inspired to admire them more and am moved to search my own soul for unadmitted flaws.

Apologize bluntly. If you were angry and harsh, go to your children and say, "I am sorry. I spoke harshly to you. That is not the way Dad should speak. Please forgive me." Apologize quickly. Go to your child that day. This prevents hurt feelings from degenerating into anger, sullenness and bitterness. Afterwards, make sure the air is clear. Ask, "Is everything all right? Is anything else bothering you?" Remember: Because you are an authority figure, they may not feel free to say everything on their mind. Help them to get it all out.

I rely on my wife to help me see my errors with the kids. Sometimes I do not realize a hurt I have caused. Geri may sense something is wrong and draw it out of them, or they may approach her with it. She then sends them to me or brings it up to me herself. I am thankful for these talks, although sometimes at first my defenses go up.

Once the apologies are made and the relationship is repaired, it is over. The issue is closed. We are free to lead again. We should move forward confidently, knowing that under God, all is well. Wallowing in guilt or losing confidence over your mistakes is not true humility—it is selfishness and lack of faith. Our families need our hand firmly back on the helm, and quickly!

The stronger men and leaders we are, the more we will need to cultivate the quality of approachability. People in our families should feel free to come to us and tell us whatever is on their minds, be it embarrassing, negative or difficult. If we blow up in anger or will not listen, then we are unapproachable. To express something negative does not necessarily mean a child has a bad attitude; to fail to express it at all will certainly create one! Never should we put our family members in this position. It is our responsibility, as the stronger one, as the leader, to create a feeling of freedom and openness in our households. If we do not, we are headed for a day of bitter reckoning.

I have been amazed at some of the things my kids needed to discuss with me, but were afraid to bring up. The subjects have ranged from guilt over past misdeeds (which may seem trivial to me) to their present struggles with the most serious temptations. They have brought me their questions, problems and insecurities. We have talked them all out. I want my children to know that I am a godly father—I will tell them the truth; I will uphold God's righteous standards, *but they can talk to me about anything, and I will listen!*

4. Have Fun, Be Hip

What's wrong with having fun? What's unspiritual about laughing until you fall out of your chair? Absolutely nothing! Holiness makes for happiness. The committed can clown around sometimes. M. Scott Peck is right when he says, "Saints must sleep and prophets must play" (*The Road Less Traveled*, p.107).

Jesus was a fun person. He went to parties. He told jokes. He nicknamed his guys ("Rocky" and "Sons of Thunder"). He loved children, and they loved him.

The Pharisees were so uptight they drove people out of the kingdom. They even rebuked Jesus for letting his disciples get too happy. Jesus did not let these lemon-souled joy stealers have their way. He responded: "...if they keep quiet, the stones will cry out" (Luke 19:40).

Children love fun people. We can always be serious when need be. It is simply a matter of knowing what mood to set. If Dad, the leader, can tell (or take!) a joke, everybody has fun. Sometimes, after a hard day, everybody just needs to laugh and kick back. If we are fun people, our kids will have fun, and if we let them have fun they will love our leadership.

Fathers need to be in tune with the current scene. You don't have to be a goof-ball older guy trying to be young (please, spare us!), but you do need to be hip to what's happening. Nerdy, out-of-touch fathers are unconnected to their children. If you are a nerd, then your kid has to make one of several decisions, all bad: (1) Humor my father but hide him from my friends, (2) become a nerd myself, (3) relate to my dad superficially since he is clueless about my real life.

We show love when we are interested in someone else's world. It demonstrates that we care enough to get inside their feelings and experiences. Paul said, "I have become all things to all men so that by all possible means I might save some" (1 Corinthians 9:22). If we are going to save our kids, then we need to take a look at the current youth scene and not ridicule it. Confront the sin but accept the style. Try to understand the music, the lingo and the clothes. We should remember what we felt and did when *we* were that age!

❧

I began this chapter by sharing with you my relationship with my father. I carry his memory in my heart and have his picture on my desk. I hold as one of my prize possessions the shotgun he presented me as he lay upon his deathbed.

I have often longed for a chance to see him again, for a time to sit and talk, to tell him all I feel, and to let him see who I have become. I have wished that I could also listen and come to know him as I never did. But it is not to be. That opportunity is no more. But I can be the father I need to be! I can lead and love my children as I should. I can seize every precious day of life I have together with them, and give my all, remembering that I have my children, and this moment, but only for a little while.

CHAPTER 3

Wife and Mother

A wife of noble character who can find? She is worth far more than rubies...Her children arise and call her blessed; her husband also, and he praises her, "Many women do noble things, but you surpass them all" (Proverbs 31:10, 28-29).

What is your concept of the ideal wife and mother? It used to be so very clear what these words "wife and mother" meant. However, as women have become "liberated" and life has become more fast-paced, traditional moral values and roles within the family have been questioned, ridiculed and all but disregarded. Most of us are confused. We desire to have great families, yet we are walking along paths that are no longer clearly defined.

But don't despair—all is not lost! You can know where you are going and how to get there. It is not easy, and certainly not simplistic, but God has left some very specific instructions to women. God is the one who created and established marriage and family. He designed family, and he knows how it is to function and how we are to fulfill our roles within it.

The ideas I will share with you are not new; they are very old ones, but in fact that is what makes them seem so new! They are almost unheard of today; when they are presented, they are often misunderstood and misapplied. The world does not grasp and has, in fact, deeply resented many of God's teachings on family. Unfortunately, many, many Christians have listened to and bought into the world's reactions (or should I say, Satan's lies?) and have paid a terrible price.

Defining the woman's role in marriage and motherhood— where do we start? Actually God has defined it rather simply. In almost every scripture referring to the role of the wife, God comes back to the basic principle of submission and adaptation. (Yes, there it is. . . the dreaded "S-word!") When the Bible discusses motherhood, it defines that role primarily as one of nurturing.

Some of us are good mothers, yet we leave much to be desired as wives. Others of us are devoted wives, but are inadequate mothers. Both of these roles must be fulfilled as God intended in order to have a happy, harmonious family life and to raise awesome children. In my experience, I have found that more women fail as supportive wives than as nurturing mothers. Most problems in family life are the result of difficulties in the marriage. We can be the world's most wonderful mothers, but if we are filled with selfishness and bitterness as wives, our children will suffer, and their lives will bear the consequences of our sin!

First, we will look at and discuss the role of submission in marriage and see how this affects our ability to be effective mothers.

Part 1

The Wife—Model of Submission

Wives, submit to your husbands as to the Lord. . .Now as
the church submits to Christ, so also wives should submit to
their husbands in everything (Ephesians 5:22, 24).

Wives, submit to your husbands as is fitting in the Lord
(Colossians 3:18).

Wives, in the same way be submissive to your husbands. .
.like Sarah, who obeyed Abraham and called him her
master. You are her daughters if you do what is right and
do not give way to fear (1 Peter 3:1, 5-6).

Then they can train the younger women to love their
husbands and children, to be self-controlled and pure, to
be busy at home, to be kind, and to be subject to their
husbands, so that no one will malign the word of God (Titus
2:4-5).

The ability to adapt and adjust to authority is one of the most
important lessons we must learn in life. Rebellion against God's
authority resulted in Satan being cast out of heaven (Revelation
12:7-9) and Adam and Eve being cast out of the Garden (Genesis
3:23). Not only must we submit to God, but to numerous other
authorities—the government, employers, parents, teachers and
coaches, to name just a few.

God uses the family unit to demonstrate and model the
principles of life that all of us must learn. By God's design so much
of life is encompassed and acted out at home—leadership, respect,
obedience, love, encouragement and the give-and-take in relationships. Get it right at home, and we will probably get it right
everywhere else!

God's plan is for the husband to lead with power and humility and for the wife to follow with strength and support. The wife has the very unique role of modeling in the flesh the role of submission, a role her children must learn if they are to succeed in life. How many children never learn to submit to legitimate authorities because they never see a healthy example at home?

My mother modeled submission for me as a child in a way more powerful than words could ever describe. It was obvious by what she said and how she said it that she deeply respected my father. I always knew that once my dad had made a decision, there would be no arguing, complaining or maneuvering around it. Because of the submission my mother demonstrated, I grew up with a healthy respect for men and other authorities and with a positive view of marriage as well.

Why have we reacted so negatively to the idea of submission? For most of us, it is because submission implies weakness and wimpiness. Unfortunately, that is often the way we have seen it applied. We have seen women who are beaten down, anxious, fearful and lacking any sense of self-esteem or self-confidence, and we have concluded that these traits are a result of submission. Nothing could be further from the truth. The word "submissive" is not and was never intended to be synonymous with "weak." Look at the examples of godly, submissive women in the Bible— they are anything but weak! Consider Sarah, Rebekah, Deborah, Abigail, Mary the mother of Jesus, Priscilla and the noble woman of Proverbs 31. These are women with passion, spunk and sparkle. They exemplify undaunted courage and strong convictions, and yet, their lives exude a spirit of submission.

Now that we are completely confused and some of us are perhaps even a little angry, let's get practical. What does it mean then to "submit," and how does a wife serve as a model of the submissive spirit to her children? Let us look at three different aspects of submission.

1. Submission: An Ordering of Relationships

People of all ages function best when the order of relationships is clearly defined. While many of us would always like to be the one in charge, life goes smoothly only when it is clearly established who is in charge and who will follow. This is true in the classroom, in business and at home. I remember one day when our oldest daughter was three and a half, she looked at me with the "Aha!" look that a child gets when he or she finally understands an important truth. She said, "I know! God is the boss of Daddy; Daddy is the boss of you; you are the boss of me. . .and I am the boss of Sunny (our 25-pound dog)!"

Yes, life works better when we understand the order of relationships! This is God's way of doing things, and we mothers need to demonstrate it practically to our children.

2. Submission: An Attitude More Than an Action

> ...and the wife must respect her husband (Ephesians 5:33).

This concept must be grasped in order to understand submission. Submission is an attitude of respect that issues from our hearts. How many of us have seen and been repulsed by women who do all the right things and yet are obviously seething with anger and disdain for their husbands? Let me ask, what does this attitude produce in the children who are watching? It produces children who begrudgingly do as they are told, but with sullenness, defiance and deceitfulness.

Respectful submission is only possible if we have the proper attitude about ourselves. "Do not think of yourselves more highly than you ought, but rather think of yourself with sober judgment ..." (Romans 12:3). Let's face it, most of us have a problem with submission because we are sure that we are right! Submission is usually not an issue until there is a disagreement or a difference

51

of opinion. Think about it—if both of you were in agreement, would there be a submission issue?

Obviously, none of us can ever compromise the will and commands of God under the guise of being submissive. Our obedience to God takes absolute precedence over any other authority in life. "We must obey God rather than men" (Acts 5:29). But, there are, and always will be, times when one of us must yield to the other. Submission does not mean we have no opinions. (I personally have opinions about almost everything!) It does mean that we are not always right and that we can willingly yield our opinions to our husband's. We must do this without resentment and without self-pity. We must submit without thinking, "I hope he's wrong," and without saying, "I told you so!" if, in fact, we prove to be right.

Why is this so important in parenting? Have you ever dealt with a child who fully believed he or she was right or with a teenager who was convinced he or she knew everything there was to know about life? As parents, we expect our children to obey and to yield to our decisions. How much easier it is for a child or a teenager to submit when they have seen that attitude continually modeled by their parents.

Submission is not a technique that we use to resolve conflict—it is a basic attitude of respect. A submissive spirit is more than a mere acquiescence in order to keep peace—it is a way of valuing our husbands. When a woman respects her husband it is obvious. He feels it; the children see and imitate it, and all the world takes notice!

3. Submission: A Way of Speaking

> If anyone considers himself religious and yet does not keep a tight rein on his tongue, he deceives himself and his religion is worthless (James 1:26).

> The tongue is a fire, a world of evil among the parts of the
> body. It corrupts the whole person, sets the whole course
> of his life on fire, and is itself set on fire by hell (James 3:6).

Words have an amazing power—power to build up or power to destroy. They can be precious gifts or hurtful weapons. How many times have we heard words flying from our mouths—words that we could not seem to stop, words that were destined to ridicule, hurt, tear down or threaten? Once released, they speed toward the target, free to wound and damage. Later we can apologize and repent. But unwise, hurtful words cannot be ignored, recaptured or ever quite forgotten. As wives and mothers we must carefully guard our speech. We must use our words to bring about good, not harm. Nowhere is a submissive spirit demonstrated more powerfully than in the way a woman uses her words.

One of my favorite women in the Bible is Abigail (1 Samuel 25). While I admire Abigail's courage and tenacity, she especially serves as a model of how to say difficult things in the right way. Submission does not always mean silence. Abigail confronted David directly, and yet, she did it with the utmost respect and concern. She exemplifies "speaking the truth in love" (Ephesians 4:15), showing us that anything that needs to be said can be said when it is spoken in the right way.

In every family there will be times when we must talk through difficult issues. As husbands and wives, we must learn to talk with one another and even to challenge one another, but keeping in mind that we are on the same side. We must speak candidly and yet with genuine love and respect. Never is there an excuse to belittle or berate each other or to speak to each other with crudeness and cursing. These are the words that kill marriages, destroy lives and ruin children! If our words are spoken with love and respect, we can say whatever must be said, solve any problem, and come out united. Just as David owed Abigail his very soul because of the things she courageously said to him, so will we help each other stay saved and make it to heaven. What greater lessons can our children learn than how to talk about difficult things openly, honestly and respectfully?

It is said of the noble woman of Proverbs 31 that "she speaks with wisdom, and faithful instruction is on her tongue" (v. 26). As a result, her children and her husband praise her (v. 28). But of another woman in Proverbs it is said, "Better to live in a desert than with a quarrelsome and ill-tempered wife" (Proverbs 21:19). What is the best description of your conversation? Is it wise and faithful or quarrelsome and ill-tempered? Nothing destroys the atmosphere of a home more than a whining, contradictory wife. A negative, complaining atmosphere robs a family of joy and peace. This kind of talk is also contagious! Are your children whiners, complainers, argumentative? Could it be they are only imitating what they see in you? The atmosphere and tone of the home rests with you, and much of it is determined by the way you speak—first, to your husband, and, second, to your children.

Part 2

The Mother as Nurturer

...but his mother treasured all these things in her heart. And Jesus grew in wisdom and stature, and in favor with God and men (Luke 2:51-52).

Just as Jesus was loved and cared for by his mother, we also must love and take care of our children. Our primary role as mother is one of nurturer. We will discuss the four main ways we must nurture our children: emotionally, physically, spiritually and socially.

1. Nurture Them Emotionally

> As a mother comforts her child, so will I comfort you. . .
> (Isaiah 66:13).

> . . .we were gentle among you like a mother caring for her
> little children (1 Thessalonians 2:7).

The entire world can be against us; life can be incredibly difficult, but all is well, in those moments when we feel a mother's love! There is nothing quite like it! It is the first relationship of love that a person experiences in this life. It is God's plan for the comfort and closeness of a mother's love to be our initial taste of this world; it prepares us for life ahead.

A special closeness

Most of us deeply love our children and, in the early months, are especially close to them. We nurse them, cuddle them and meet their every need. Yet, as those babies grow older, we can lose the special closeness of infancy. An intimate relationship with our children must continually be cultivated. This relationship will convince them that they are valuable human beings even when the world tries to make them feel worthless. It will serve as a solid bulwark against the inevitable ups and downs of life as they make their way out into the world.

Learn how to be a warm, affectionate person. Touch your children, hug them, smile at them, encourage them with your words. Tell them over and over again how much you love them! I often say to Alexandra, my youngest, "Do you know how much I love you?" She answers with the expression I have told her for years, " More than all the world and everything that is in it!"

I realized long ago, as we first began to raise our children, how very much I did not know and how many times I made mistakes. I held on to a scripture then and still rely on it today (especially now that two of our children are teenagers!): "Above all, love each other deeply, because love covers a multitude of sins" (1 Peter 4:8). I decided then—I will probably make plenty of mistakes, but my children will never doubt how much I love them and believe in them. I am sure that my love has protected them many times from my imperfections as a parent!

A special relationship

Not only must there be the emotional bond of love and affection with our children, but there must be a unique relationship with each of them as individuals.

Every child is a unique creation of God. He broke the mold after making each one! Each of your children must hold a very special place in your heart that can be filled by no one else! What if God loved us deeply, but only *en masse?* Thankfully, he loves us individually. Each of us has a special place in his heart. He knows us, loves us, and "likes" us. He knows the number of hairs on our heads and has our own room in heaven prepared especially for us!

I thought for years that I was my mother's favorite daughter until as an adult I discovered that all three of my sisters were convinced of the same thing about themselves! It was not that my mom told any one of us that she was loved more than the others. No, it was just the way she loved us as individuals and made all of us feel uniquely valued and appreciated. We all grew up believing we were special and knowing we were deeply loved! Now that is the work of a great mother!

From oldest to youngest, from similar personalities to exact opposites, our children must feel bonded in heart to us. In one sense, we must love each of them "the most" because each adds something to our lives that no one else does. The more children you have and the busier life becomes, the more difficult this will be.

Our family experienced a wake-up call in this area several years ago. The first three of our children were born fairly close together and the fourth, Alexandra, followed six years later. By the time Alexandra was born, the other children were busy in school, and I had begun working full time in the ministry. Because of the demands on our schedule, we hired someone to help us at home. Although I thoroughly enjoyed Alexandra I did not realize until several years later that I was not as close to her emotionally (nor she to me) as I had been to the others. We eventually moved and the person whom Alexandra had come to love so much no longer worked for us. The weakness in our relationship was exposed. Alexandra changed from an active, joyful toddler to a quiet little girl. She cried easily and no longer enjoyed school. I checked everything—her health, her school, her friends, her schedule. None of those things were the problem. Finally, Sam said he felt the problem was that she just did not feel close to me! After dealing with my guilt, regret and pride, I went to work on my relationship with Alexandra. I spent more time with her, talked more to her, and listened attentively when she talked to me. (It is so easy not to be attentive to a four-year-old when you have three older children clamoring to talk about seemingly more important things!) I am happy to say that the improvements in her behavior came quickly and were dramatic.

I am so thankful that the problem was exposed as it was and when it was. It frightens me to think of the direction Alexandra's life could have taken, as well as the relationship and friendship with her that might never have been mine, had this not changed. She is a very special little girl, a gift from God and today, at six years old, is full of love and life. More than loving her, I am close to her. I know her, and I like her. She has a strong will that requires a firm hand, but now we have the relationship needed to take her through childhood and on into life!

A special understanding

Without an understanding of our children as individuals, it is impossible to train and mold them adequately. Too many parents love their children but honestly do not know or understand them. How can you "train a child in the way he should go" (Proverbs 22:6) when you do not know where he or she is coming from?

God, the perfect example of parenthood, loves us and knows us, intimately and individually.

> "Oh Lord, you have searched me
> > and you know me.
> You know when I sit and when I rise;
> > You perceive my thoughts from afar.
> You discern my going out and my lying down;
> > You are familiar with all my ways.
> Before a word is on my tongue
> > you know it completely, O Lord.
> Where can I go from your Spirit?
> > Where can I flee from your presence?
> Even there your hand will guide me,
> > your right hand will hold me fast"
> > (Psalm 139:1-4,7,10).

Mothers, study your children. Discover their abilities and talents and learn their character strengths. Build up, encourage and develop these areas of their lives. What are their weaknesses? Are there weaknesses of ability or proficiency that you can help strengthen? What are their character flaws that left undealt with will destroy them as adults? Is there laziness, deceitfulness, selfishness, uncontrolled anger? If we would only nurture our children's characters as zealously as we encourage their mental capacities and athletic abilities, we would raise awesome kids.

I don't understand it—maybe it comes from the nine months of pregnancy in which we shared the same body; perhaps it is woman's intuition; maybe it is just the enhanced sensitivity that is a part of love. But I do believe God gives mothers a unique ability to sense the needs and to draw out the feelings of children. We may be the one who first senses hurt feelings, anger or bad attitudes. We also may be the first to realize that there is a more serious problem. Mothers, we must watch, listen, pay attention and deal with what we see.

On the other hand, never undermine your children's relationship with their dad. Often it is easier to talk to Mom. We may seem softer and less intimidating, or perhaps we see needs more quickly. This is understandable, but it should never lead to a situation where Mom and the kids are close and talk freely, but Dad is kept in the dark. Encourage and insist that your children learn to talk to their father, especially as they get older. In our family, the children have a very healthy respect for their dad. They love and admire Sam greatly, yet sometimes have been afraid of what he would say or think. Especially when they were younger, it was much easier for them to come to me. I worked very hard to help them feel free to talk to their father and never allowed myself to be in the middle of a strained or awkward relationship.

It takes work to nurture your children emotionally. Some of you may be feeling quite overwhelmed. Let me give you some practical advice that can help:

● **Make use of the little periods of time.** Throughout the day, grasp the minutes here and there to talk with and draw near to your children. As they get older, this will be even more important because small amounts of time will often be all you will have.

● **Take one with you!** Ever since our third child was born and we were outnumbered by children, Sam and I have made it our practice to take a child with us whenever possible as we run errands. Instead of being "dead" time, grocery shopping, banking, etc. can be spent enjoying the company of our children.

● **Consider chauffeuring a blessing from God!** I have sometimes thought that I should put my entire house on wheels since I seem to be living in the car, chauffeuring children to and from school and countless activities. If we let it, this can be one of the most frustrating parts of motherhood. We are always in the car! Yet, we probably should count it as one of God's real blessings to our lives. The time I spend in the car each day has provided some of the best time to talk with our older children. Not only does it allow us to talk about things they may be troubled by, tempted with or excited about, but it gives me the chance to give guidance and input to situations just as they get ready to meet them. I often drop them off and pray all the way home about the things I've just heard! Also, driving them places with their friends enables me to overhear conversations and understand the mindset of other kids.

● **Make bedtimes special.** Spend a few minutes at bedtime talking about the day. Sometimes children need to talk about their feelings—hurt, disappointment, anger, joy. At other times they need to confess sins and clear their consciences before us and before God. (All of us know how much better is the sleep of a clear conscience!) And at every bedtime, love can be expressed with words and with touch; whether it be hugs and kisses or a light caress, a gentle squeeze or a loving pat. The last thing I want my children to know before they close their eyes at night is that I love them with all my heart.

2. Nurture Them Physically

"She is like the merchant ships,
          bringing her food from afar.
She gets up while it is still dark;
          she provides food for her family
          and portions for her servant girls.

"When it snows, she has no fear for her household;
　　　for all of them are clothed in scarlet.
She makes coverings for her bed;
　　　she is clothed in fine linen and purple"
　　　(Proverbs 31:14-15, 21-22).

As do all mothers, I cherish every card, letter and hand-made gift my children have given to me. Their expressions of devotion move me to tears and also bring smiles to my face. The things they thank us for are the things that are most important to them. Not long ago, Jonathan wrote me a card for Valentine's Day. I share with you just as he wrote it, "Who knows where the family'd be without you? We'd have bad food, always be late for school, unhappy. We'd be a mess!"

So much of nurturing a child is providing for his or her physical needs. It takes an incredible amount of time and energy to run a household and take care of our families. On top of all of this, many of us mothers are juggling a full-time job outside the home. Regardless of how demanding our jobs are or how busy our schedules, if we have children, then we must take care of them!

Children need to be fed decent, nourishing meals at regular times. (In a later chapter we will deal more with the importance of eating meals together as families.) Some of us are so busy that our meals too often consist of snacks or fast-food stops. There is nothing wrong with occasionally eating pizza or fast-food hamburgers (our family loves these times!). But as mothers we are given the job of providing nourishing meals for our families and we need to do it!

We do not need to be short-order cooks, preparing a different food for every family member according to his or her taste or desire that particular day. Children are often picky eaters. The best way to handle "pickiness" is to not make it a big deal! I have always tried to have at least one thing I knew a picky eater would like. If they eat only that one thing but nothing else, I do not expect anything more than that they try one taste of the other things. I do not go back to the stove preparing two or three other tasty treats for the one with the delicate taste buds. I have seen mothers worrying so much over what their little ones were or were not eating that they actually created an eating problem! Most children get what they need as long as we don't fill them up with junk food. Young children will have meals where they eat some foods and hardly touch others. David, my most finicky eater, when he was young, usually ate everything in sight at breakfast, a small amount of lunch and almost nothing at dinner. He loved white rice so we had many meals that included rice. We did not overreact and needless to say, David lived and grew. He now eats more than anyone else in our family!

On the other hand, undisciplined eating creates problems that can last into adulthood. Growing children may need snacks several times a day in addition to regular nutritious meals, but they should not eat uncontrollably or indiscriminately. In our family, we have never allowed our children unlimited access to snack foods. They are not free to "graze" through the kitchen all day long. Too many children are overweight and physically unfit. Often these same children struggle with a weak, self-indulgent character. Help them while they are young to establish disciplined eating habits and healthy attitudes about food.

Aside from the challenges of feeding a growing family, our job is to make sure our children are clothed properly. This can be quite a challenge, both to our schedules and to our bank accounts. After recently buying four pairs of shoes in one day, I was reminded again of the financial challenge of clothing a family!

We must have a godly focus on the physical needs of life. Women, especially, must keep a balanced perspective. Because we are the ones who take care of so many of the physical needs of our families, we spend more time in the stores and are confronted with the glitz and glamour of things! The physical needs of life are legitimate and important, but they must never become our focus or take the place of the things that really matter. Mothers, our attitudes on these things will be imitated by our children. If we are consumed with external appearances and material things, they will be also! If our attitudes are healthy and spiritual, these same attitudes will be reflected in our children.

> "...Is not life more important than...clothes?...So do not worry saying, 'What shall we eat?' or 'What shall we wear?' For the pagans run after all these things, and your heavenly Father knows that you need them. But seek first his kingdom and his righteousness and all of these things will be given to you as well" (Matthew 6:25, 31-33).

Now that I've said all of this, let me say that it is important to help our children dress and carry themselves in such a way as to relate with and be accepted by other people, especially their peers. Some children are more concerned with their appearance than others. As a teacher, I know that the neatness, cleanliness and attractiveness of children does affect their behavior and, like it or not, the way they are treated by their teachers and their peers.

If your children have no idea what looks good, help them. Just make sure your own ideas of what is attractive are coming out of today and not the 1960s! I spoke with a mother not long ago concerning her 12-year-old son. He was often ridiculed by other kids. He was called names and put down repeatedly on the bus and at school. As I got to know this boy, I realized that he had a great heart and a likeable personality, but it was difficult to get past his appearance. He always looked sloppy, out-dated and slightly effeminate. While some of us could see beyond this and like him as a person, the children at school (and many adults as well) were never going to give this kid a chance. I spoke to his mother about getting him a professional hair cut (Mom had been his barber) and helping him dress better. He showed up at church several days later with a new hair cut and "lookin' good"! He obviously felt like a new man!

Mothers, you do not have to spend large amounts of money or dress your children like models, but it is your job to help them look good and be relatable. Appearance is only external but it is the first thing people see. If we fail to dress our children within reasonable limits of fashion and neatness, we do our children a grave disservice.

Let me say one more thing regarding physical needs and appearance. It matters to children how their parents look! They want to be proud of us when they introduce us to their friends or, heaven forbid, when they are seen with us! As I said earlier, we do not have to become obsessed with our appearances, but we do need to do the best we can with what we've got. Mothers, as we get older, we will have to put some effort into staying in shape (or getting there to begin with!). We will not only look better, but will have more energy. We need to put on make-up, style our hair, and dress attractively. We will have a better attitude about life and our children will have a better attitude about us!

3. Nurture Them Spiritually

When our children are small, we probably will be the primary person to demonstrate and teach them a genuine, live faith. We usually spend more time with young children, especially if we are able to be at home with them.

Beginning when they are very young, we can teach our children that God loves them, and we can help them to love him back. "We love God because he first loved us" (1 John 4:19). Love for God begins with a heart-felt appreciation for all that he is, all he has done and all he has given. Gratitude does not necessarily come naturally to children—it must be taught and explained.

Chapter 7 will be devoted to the spiritual training of children, but let me discuss a few specifics for mothers of younger children:

Teach them to love God through nature

When was the last time you noticed the beauty of God's sunrise or sunset? When did you last marvel at the power of God in the pounding surf or at his magnificence in the vivid colors of autumn? To this day, when my own faith weakens or falters, I go back to the God I know from nature. I look around at the beauty, power and intricacy of creation, and I always come back to the same truth: Only a God powerful enough to be Lord could have done all of this. "For since the creation of the world God's invisible qualities—his eternal power and divine nature—have been clearly seen, being understood from what has been made..." (Romans 1:20).

Help your children develop a real awareness of and love for what God has made. Show them, tell them, and teach them the magic of God's creation. I believe a child who deeply loves and appreciates what God has made will, like David of the Bible, grow up to be a man or woman after God's own heart.

Teach them by our lives

It's plain and simple—"actions speak louder than words." Our children need to see that we really believe that God is our Father and that Jesus is our Savior! They need to see that we have a genuine relationship with him, and it affects every part of our lives. I remember overhearing Elizabeth, when she was quite young, telling a friend, "My mom prays a lot." Do our children see that God is real in our lives? Do they know that we pray and talk to him? Do they see us reading the Bible and allowing God's words to guide our lives? God will be as real to our children as he is to us. If our religion is mere talk, doctrine or a harsh taskmaster, so it will be for them!

Teach them with the Scriptures

> But as for you, continue in what you have learned and have become convinced of, because you know those from whom you learned, and how from infancy you have known the holy Scriptures, which are able to make you wise for salvation through faith in Christ Jesus. All Scripture is God-breathed and is useful for teaching, rebuking, correcting and training in righteousness, so that the man of God may be thoroughly equipped for every good work (2 Timothy 3:14-16).

I believe with all my heart that the Bible is from God and provides answers and guidance to any situation. I believe that when the Bible is obeyed and its principles or commands followed, they always work. But what has amazed me is the power of God's word to change my children! I have said things over and over again to my children with little response and much frustration. Can you relate? I have also used the Bible to teach the very same things and my children have responded eagerly and immediately! I do not understand it except to say that the Bible is "living and active" (Hebrews 4:12) and, more than any other book, the Bible is your best resource. It helps the children to realize that there is a standard over both of us. It is not just Mom saying to obey; God wants Mom and us to obey him."

Use the scriptures to mold character and to teach your children the truths about life! You can find a scripture or an example to help you deal with any situation, any problem, any attitude. Here are some particular situations you may need to deal with and the scriptures that we have used with our children:

Jealousy - Genesis 4:4-9

At five years old, Elizabeth was quite jealous of David. One day I exasperatedly read this scripture about Cain and Abel to her, a little unsure if it might be too strong. She thought about it, looked at me and said, "I wonder if they didn't like each other when they were little?" She got it!

Sibling Relationships - Exodus 2:1-10

In the story of Miriam and Moses is a great example of an older sibling taking care of a younger brother or sister.

James 4:1-2

Do you have children who are constantly quarrelling or who don't get along? The real problem is that they both want their own way.

Whining and Complaining - Philippians 4:4

This is one of the first scriptures our children memorized when they were unhappy and whining. Again, the special power of the Scriptures: When we would begin to say this scripture and have Elizabeth say it with us, she would always burst out laughing!

Philippians 2:14-15

Encourage them to want to "shine like stars." Alexandra loved this scripture. She, like many of us, responds best when she is inspired to be better.

Worrying and Fretting - Philippians 4:6-7

This is a wonderful scripture to teach them how to deal with things that cause them anxiety.

> - pray about everything
> - be thankful

This was a favorite of David's. He was a worrier. We would talk about this scripture, memorize it, and pray for "peace in his heart."

Anger - Ephesians 4:25-27

Some children have a more emotional, volatile nature. They must learn to deal with things that bother them before their emotions get out of control. Jonathan struggled with his temper, and this scripture helped him tremendously. He learned to talk about what he was feeling instead of blowing up.

Laziness - Proverbs 6:6-8

Do you have a child who is content to watch everyone else carry the whole load? Deal with this while they are young! Be hard-line, and insist on hard work, but whenever possible, make it fun. Our motto for Jonathan several years ago was "be a lover of hard work."

Love - 1 Corinthians 13:4-7

The most important quality in any of our lives is love. We must actively teach our children to be loving, caring people. This is a great verse to memorize.

There are so many other scriptures that can be used powerfully to inspire our children, to build their faith, and to shape their character. Use the Bible. Let it "dwell in you richly" (Colossians 3:16) as you teach your children. Every principle of righteousness that you need to teach them and to answer their questions about life can be found in the Word. Use it!

4. Nurture Them Socially

> And Jesus grew. . .in favor with God and man (Luke 2:52).

Jesus was the greatest man who ever lived. He accomplished great things for God, brought us salvation, and lived an amazing life. Yet part of the power of his life was his ability to relate to people.

As mothers we must teach our children the social skills that enable them to get along with people and to develop healthy, meaningful relationships. The most basic of these used to be taught and expected of all children, yet they seem to be forgotten in the '90s.

Teach good manners

- Whatever happened to the magic words, "please" and "thank you"? They still carry some magic. Teach them.
- How about "excuse me" or "pardon me"?
- Teach them how to properly introduce friends and family.
- Teach them not to interrupt when others are speaking.
- Teach them not to answer in monosyllabic grunts like "yeah," "nah," "huh" and/or "un-uh." Even a polite "yes" or "no" is better.
- Do our children know that it is respectful to offer adults, especially women, seats in a crowded room?
- Are we teaching our boys that it is still good manners to open and hold doors for women?
- Are we expecting our children to look for ways to help people when they see needs: carrying packages, assisting elderly people or helping with small children, etc.?

There are hundreds of other expressions of politeness and good manners ranging from table manners to phone etiquette. All of these demonstrate attitudes of respect and consideration to other people. Above all, we must teach our children to be courteous, helpful and to be aware of the feelings and needs of other people. This not only develops their characters, but makes them much more attractive to everyone they meet.

Teach friendliness

Mothers, we must teach our children to be friendly. Teach them to greet people with warmth and smiles rather than sullen disinterest. Help them look people confidently in the eyes instead of down at their feet. Practice it together if necessary until they get it right.

Teach your children to be aware of new kids in their schools, at church and in their neighborhoods. Help them to overcome their own shyness and awkwardness and reach out to other people. We may need to help them learn how to initiate conversations. Nothing is so awkward or embarrassing as not knowing what to say. We've helped our children learn how to show interest and put others at ease in conversation. Teach them how to be warm and how to be a friend, then they will never be lacking for friends themselves.

❦

How can we adequately describe all that it means to be a mother? As we hear the word "mother," so many images flood our minds and so many feelings fill our hearts: a young mother holding a small infant, a mother standing by a stove in the kitchen, a tired woman surrounded by a mountain of laundry, and bedtime memories so vivid we can almost feel the cool hand caressing our brow and once again hear a voice saying softly, "Good night."

Say the word "mother" and our thoughts may be like a beautiful water-color—soft and peaceful. Say it again and perhaps we see the other side of motherhood—noise, confusion, feelings of exasperation and inadequacy.

Motherhood brings out the best and the worst in all who have joined its ranks. Above all, it is a privilege and a gift given by God. If we do it his way, he will provide all that we need to get the job done right. My deepest desire is that it will one day be said of us:

> Her children rise and call her blessed; her husband also, and he praises her: "Many women do noble things, but you surpass them all" (Proverbs 31:28-29).

CHAPTER 4

New Mothers

*But women will be saved through childbearing—
if they continue in faith, love and holiness with propriety (1
Timothy 2:15).*

THE BIRTH OF A CHILD IS ONE OF THE GREATEST MIRACLES OF LIFE. How utterly amazing it is to look at a tiny newborn who just a short time before was a part of your own body—a little being who had been growing within you for months, who already had brought about so many changes in your life—physically, emotionally and oh, so hormonally! Now here it is, *a baby*—a real, live, human being with two eyes, a nose, a mouth and tiny little fingers and toes. Can anything prepare you for the emotions that run through you as a new parent? They range from utter amazement at the power and creativity of God, to an unfathomable joy and immeasurable sense of love—and then, so often, just a few days later, to another emotion...one of overwhelming panic. You find yourself asking, "What have we done?" and "What do we do now?"

All of our lives have pointed toward this time, yet so many of us finally arrive at motherhood and find ourselves quite unprepared. We are filled with anxieties and insecurities in caring for and raising this seemingly helpless, frail baby. We live with an exhaustion that cannot be anticipated or described until it has been personally experienced. We have feelings of frustration, confusion and sometimes disappointment. Even a marriage that has been close and loving and quite compatible suddenly can go through a time of strain and distance. None of us will experience exactly the same difficulties, but believe me, we *all* will be tested! Sound pretty discouraging? Although raising children *is* one of the most challenging and demanding things we will ever do, it is absolutely one of the most fulfilling.

I cannot explain here all that Paul meant when he wrote our theme scripture, 1 Timothy 2:15—obviously there is much more than what I will apply—but I do believe that bearing and raising children is undeniably one of God's greatest ways of developing and refining our characters as women. Rearing children will expose weaknesses that we must conquer and will produce opportunities to mature as nothing else will.

There are so many experiences to be had and adjustments to be made as a new mother. I've been through "the new baby" four times now. Honestly, the first time around was the most difficult for me. It was all so different and so unexpected. I simply had no idea how completely my life would change with the arrival of my first child!

The major adjustments that come with motherhood are in the areas of *time, marriage and spirituality.* You will confront others to be sure, but if you deal with these, you can handle the rest.

Time Adjustment

Every time I had a baby, I was amazed at how one tiny six- or seven-pound baby could put my entire life, and my household as well, into such total chaos! The baby couldn't walk, couldn't talk, mostly ate and slept, and yet if anyone were to innocently ask me, "What did you do all day?", I would have to honestly tell them, "I don't know, but I haven't eaten, haven't gotten dressed, haven't made my bed, and I'm completely and utterly exhausted!" And yet, as out-of-control as things were initially, it was possible to gain some semblance of order in my life...and you can too.

> Be careful, then, how you live—not as unwise but as wise, making the most of every opportunity, because the days are evil (Ephesians 5:15-16) .

Be patient

It gets easier! Six months from now you will step back and smile as you see yourself juggling (and I mean literally "juggling") so many more things in your life with ease. You will learn and you will get better at it.

Be organized and flexible

The reason life is thrown into such confusion after having a baby is that most of us are not used to the constant interruptions that a newborn brings. We've got to learn how to alter our activities when our baby needs us, and yet organize our lives in such a way as to still accomplish other things as well.

We must establish a rhythm and pattern in our lives. God is a God of order and we are made in his image. Just as there is a definite pattern to creation so we also are made to thrive on order in our lives.

Even babies have a need for routine. Have you ever noticed a child's sense of timing? Babies wake up to be fed at regular intervals. As they get older, children know instinctively when it is time for lunch or their favorite TV program. I have found that the more strong-willed, emotional, and intense the child, the more important it is to provide routine for things like eating, sleeping and bathing. Watch for the signs of his or her natural body-clock and try to schedule the baby's life, and yours, around it.

Babies and children need a regular bedtime. It should not be different every night. I am convinced that many young children who seem to be completely out of control are actually in desperate need of some predictability in their helpless little lives. If you are putting them to bed whenever you happen to get around to it each night, then you, and they, will pay the price. Establish a routine. You will have calmer, happier children and a much more peaceful home!

On the other hand, children can be amazingly flexible when there is the inevitable change in routine. They won't die if awakened from a nap. They will not automatically become sick because they go to bed late one night. In fact, while I believe very much in the need for routine, I just as fervently believe that all of us must learn to adjust to the unexpected happenings of life! We helped our young children to become more flexible by putting them down to sleep in other places besides our home. Each one of them had his or her own blanket or comforter which I carried with me. If they needed a nap and we could not be home, I could still put them to sleep with the familiarity of their own blanket. They also had a special song of their own that I always sang when putting them to bed. Elizabeth loved "Silent Night" and "Now the Day is Over." Jonathan and Alexandra chose "Jesus Loves Me" (each preferred a different verse), and David, for some unknown reason, insisted on "Baa Baa Black Sheep." To each his own! If we were away from home or if someone else had to put them to bed, I or the baby sitter could sing the song and bedtime was essentially the same. In this way, I brought some flexibility into the routine I had established.

Learn to work around the "good times" and "fussy times." Often a young baby is happy and contented in the morning. He or she may take longer naps and require less attention. Use this time to get as much done as possible. This is when you can have your quiet time, take care of the house, and spend time with other people. If your baby has a particularly difficult time of day (often it will be in the late afternoon), plan your schedule accordingly. Many babies love to ride in the car and will immediately calm down and even go to sleep as soon as the engine starts. This may be when you want to go out and do errands. Or, if your baby enjoys bath time, switch it to this usually unpleasant part of the day. Above all, think! Be creative, be positive and be solution-oriented!

When David was a baby he would get irritable in the late afternoon. However, I noticed that he loved the brightness of the tile, lights and chrome in the bathroom. He would get very quiet, almost mesmerized, whenever I took him in there. I often would put him in his infant carrier, place him on the floor in the middle of the bathroom with all the lights on, and run to start dinner. I could usually count on 10 to 20 minutes of working with both hands before he would start up again! Be a wise woman—watch for what works, and keep on doing it!

Accept the fact that you probably won't ever feel like everything is finished or done perfectly

This has to be one of the most difficult things for many new parents to accept. Pray that you will do the most important things for that day. Do the very best you can, be thankful for what you did accomplish and start again tomorrow. Be patient with yourself—as time goes by, you will handle more and more!

Make the most of short periods of time

It takes less than 20 minutes to meet or visit a neighbor, write a card, call a friend or new acquaintance, or fold a basket full of laundry. Learn to exploit the short blocks of time, rather than waiting for the large amounts that never seem to come.

Simplify

Take added pressures off whenever possible. Prepare easy meals. An especially difficult day is not the time for a four-course gourmet dinner! Plan out your menus earlier in the day. Don't wait until after you have had a baby screaming for two hours to try to come up with a great idea for dinner.

Be hospitable. You can still reach out to other people, but you may need to simplify. When cooking, make two and freeze one. Order pizza occasionally. Can't handle company for dinner? Have them over for dessert and coffee instead.

Operate more from the home

For some of us, home has been more of a rest stop, a place where we go to sleep and freshen up before leaving again. With a new baby, it's not quite so easy to "pick up and go" as before. Titus 2:4-5 says "train the younger women to love their husbands and children, to be self-controlled and pure, *to be busy at home*, to be kind, and to be subject to their husbands, so that no one will malign the word of God" (emphasis mine). Learn not to just *stay home*, but to be *busy at home*. We need to spend more time in our neighborhoods, to have more people into our homes, and let our evangelism be focused where we live. We don't realize how much more is seen, how much brighter our lights shine as Christians, when people can see us as we really are, in our own homes!!

If you must work, don't fight it–accept it

I believe, if at all possible, it is best for a mother to be home with her young children to care for them, to train them, and to enjoy a time that goes by all too quickly. If your lifestyle can be adjusted and enough income brought in on one salary, then please, stay home with your young children! If a mother can work part time, allowing her more time at home with her children, she should do so! However, if it is *not* possible—and there are so many families where it is not—you must not resent and resist something that you cannot change. You will waste valuable time, and you will steal from your family what they need most from you: your love, your joy and your peace. The time you spend fretting over your time away from your children will be better used planning, organizing and doing the work of running a busy schedule and life—and loving your husband and children.

If you cannot change it, accept it and learn to do it and do it well. God thinks you can succeed or there would be a way out!

Marriage Adjustment

...and do not forsake your mother's teaching. They will be a garland to grace your head and a chain to adorn your neck (Proverbs 1:8-9).

I thank God every day for allowing me to be raised by the parents he gave me. I have truly been blessed, not only with love and support, but with some incredible examples and teachings that have been indelibly imprinted on my heart. I'm sure as my mother said some things over and over again, she must have wondered if I was really "getting it." Those things that I did "get" have truly been "garlands to grace my head" and "chains that have adorned my neck." How many times did she say, "Geri, don't be so loud;" "Geri, don't be so bossy" (still a tough one!); "Pretty is as pretty does;" and "God must always be first in your life." These are the teachings I still remember vividly. Some have refined my life; others have become the foundation.

But there was another truth that my mother taught and modeled for all four of her children: "You are a wife first and a mother second. Your children will grow up and leave, but your husband is with you forever." Seeing this put into practice in my home as I grew up, and even more—knowing that this is God's plan—carried us through some of the toughest adjustments of our marriage. Some go through hard times in the year or so after a new marriage, but for many others, the birth of a baby brings the first great challenges to what has been a solid, loving marriage. In so many marriages, pregnancy and the birth of a first child is when love cools and is never rekindled. No one could have prepared me for the new and unexpected intensity of a mother's love for her baby. It is an emotion given by God—but it must be used in a godly way! Yet, so often, in the unexpected intensity of love that a new mother has for her baby, the emotions of warmth, love, and even "need" for her husband fades. He can be completely shut out or treated like a hired hand—there for your convenience, to do your bidding. Sounds terrible—but I have seen it over and over again in Christian marriages. It is wrong, it is ungodly, and it will hurt your child's future more than you can know!

Emotions and feelings come and go. They may be great, but they cannot be treated as facts; they must be under the control of what is righteous and true. Decide to believe and act on fact and godly truths, and the right feelings and emotions will follow.

Decide that you will love your husband first and forever.

Decide now that you *both* are the parents! This is not "your baby," "my baby" . . . this is "our baby." I've seen so many young mothers consumed with the baby and its needs, treating the new young fathers as mere appendages to the family who know nothing and can do nothing right. Nothing could be more destructive to your marriage as well as to the future relationship of respect and admiration your child needs to have with his or her father.

Decide to be close emotionally and sexually—"and the two will become one flesh" (Matthew 19:5). Decide to be warm and expressive and affectionate, not distant and preoccupied. So many couples who had enjoyed an exciting and fulfilling sexual relationship before pregnancy never seem to get back to that point, much less take it higher after childbirth. For many women, dealing with the physical satisfaction of nursing and cuddling an infant, not to mention what appears to be irreparable damage to her figure, causes her sexual desires to drop to almost nothing. While that may be what you feel—or should I say, don't feel—you've got to *fight* to get that part of your marriage back on track. You need to be functioning as one flesh as soon as possible after the birth of your baby—usually within four to six weeks. You may not think you have much sexual desire, but you do need the closeness and intimacy of the sexual relationship. You need it, your husband needs it. A dead physical desire will be awakened only with time, love and perseverance, not by waiting for lightning to strike as the two of you drift farther and farther apart from each other. You are not crazy, you are not abnormal; it will not be this way forever—but for now, you may have to *work* at awakening the romantic love between you!

Spiritual Adjustment

> Unless the Lord builds the house, its builders labor in vain...Sons are a heritage from the Lord, children a reward from him (Psalm 127:1, 3).

I remember reading an article years ago describing something done in the new fathers' waiting room of a hospital. A box was set out, inviting each new father to contribute the thoughts and reactions he experienced during the time of childbirth. As I read the notes reprinted in the magazine, I was moved as, almost without exception, these men talked about their renewed faith in a powerful Creator and a deep sense of reverence and gratitude for God. I couldn't help but wonder what happened to those moments of moving faith and spiritual insight in the weeks and months that followed.

Children are among God's most wonderful and amazing blessings. It is impossible to look upon the miracle of a new baby and not feel a renewed sense of awe and faith in the power of an Almighty Creator. And yet, for so many Christians, the birth of a baby and the beginning of a family marks that time in life of a gradual spiritual decline. This is when they become weak spiritually, more and more consumed with self and the world, never to recover and be as strong and productive as they once were. As a result, God's greatest blessing has become one of Satan's most insidious weapons to kill us spiritually.

You don't have to plummet spiritually now that you are a mother. It doesn't have to happen! God's plan and desire is that childbirth will not destroy us spiritually, but in fact, help us to be saved!

Let me remind you, having a baby is a tremendous adjustment in every way, in every area of your life. You will have to make spiritual adjustments. It will take determination to maintain a deep, meaningful and growing walk with God. Our relationship with God is a relationship of love and commitment and faith. Just as the closeness between husband and wife is tested and must be fought for, so also we must fight to stay close to the Lord.

Don't be surprised at the "spiritual slump" you may find yourself in. But do not allow yourself to stay there! Often the most distressing thing to deal with is a feeling of sluggishness and lack of motivation, as well as a sense of let-down and even depression. Some women experience this to a greater degree than others. One young Christian mother described it well as "the baby fog." Understand that much of this is the result of fatigue and hormones that are completely out of balance. Realize it, accept it, but on the other hand, fight and make every effort to "get it back." "Never be lacking in zeal, but keep your spiritual fervor, serving the Lord" (Romans 12:11). Sometimes you just have to *do* what is right, giving and serving; your emotions and zeal will come back. James 4:7-8 says, "Submit yourselves, then, to God. Resist the devil, and he will flee from you. Come near to God and he will come near to you."

Let me give you a few practicals that may help you to prevent or overcome a spiritual slump:

1. Get as much rest as you can in the first few weeks following childbirth. Don't try to be superwoman. Let your body recover and get to know your new baby. But don't become overly preoccupied with yourself, either!

2. Maintain a personal relationship with the Lord—whether you feel close to him or not — "in season or out"! Try different times for your quiet time until you find what works best: early mornings, after your husband leaves, early afternoon when the children are napping.

Use feeding times to pray and meditate. Be realistic. It is better to consistently spend 20 to 30 minutes with God every day than to unrealistically try to find an hour that may not be there. Lengthen the time as you can. Above all, *be consistent.*

3. Take advantage of new opportunities. Your baby is the greatest evangelistic tool you will ever have. Everyone loves babies. People will never be so easy to meet! But, do talk about more than just *your* baby and *yourself*!

4. Stay involved in the body, the church, even if you feel "out of it"! Use the telephone to keep in touch with other people. It's amazing all you can do while cradling a phone to your neck! I have become great at nursing a hungry baby, preparing dinner, and mopping up spills with my foot, all while carrying on a somewhat meaningful conversation on the telephone!

Come to services and functions of the church. Babies are flexible. They can go places. They can miss occasional naps. You can even leave them at times with other reliable people. Honestly, this is harder on you, the new mother, than on the baby!

It takes planning and perseverance. Remember, Satan is at work trying to sabotage your efforts to grow spiritually. Decide, "I need to be there." Plan and allow *plenty* of time for the unexpected, which will always happen just before you must leave. You will have to allow much more time to get ready than you used to. When my first three children were small, I had to get up by 4:30 or 5 a.m. on Sunday so I could arrive by 9. It was hard but absolutely worth it.

5. Get advice from mature, spiritual women. Let them help you decide about sickness—when to take your baby out and when to leave him or her at home. I don't believe in exposing healthy children to sicknesses or in dragging sick children around, but I also know that some young children live with slight sniffles most of their lives, yet are not contagious or really sick. Get help and advice!

Ask other Christians, "Am I doing too much, pushing too hard, or could I—should I—be doing more?"

Cherish the Time

As I conclude this chapter for new mothers, let me urge you—enjoy your children! Watch everything they do with joy, pride and amazement. You are watching a miracle of God unfold before your very eyes. Appreciate it, enjoy it, and revel in the mystery of it! Ironically, just as we begin to feel confident in handling our infant, it turns into...a TODDLER!

I vividly remember when, on Elizabeth's third birthday, she went up to her father and said, "Daddy, when will I be two again?" I still remember the look Sam and I gave each other as we told her, "Never, honey...you'll never be two again." I write these words a few days before that same little girl turns 17. One year more and she will turn 18, leaving for college and a life of her own.

What happened to that tiny little girl, the one who kept me up so many nights as a newborn, the two-year-old who challenged my authority (and my confidence) as no one ever had, the four-year- old who, when she didn't get her way, threatened, "I won't be your best friend!"? Yet today, she is indeed my best friend.

What happened to the years? They have flown by so quickly. I remember feeding her her first cereal as she sat in her infant seat and singing "Sunrise, Sunset" to her because, even then, I had a deep sense of how short that time would be. And now, it surely won't be long before she has babes of her own. Young mothers, cherish this time, laugh at the craziness of it, cry at the shortness, remember all you can, and, above all, let these days and weeks and years be the time for God to mold and shape you into all you were meant to be.

FUNDAMENTALS

5

The Four Essentials

These commandments that I give you today are to be upon your hearts. Impress them on your children. Talk about them when you sit at home and when you walk along the road, when you lie down and when you get up (Deuteronomy 6:6,7).

WHATEVER ELSE YOU MAY LEARN FROM THIS BOOK, LEARN THIS chapter! These principles are the basics, the critical essentials. They need to be second-nature in your parenting. The four essentials are: love, respect, obedience and honesty. We will discuss each one thoroughly.

The First Essential: Love

Jesus was asked once which was the most important commandment of all. Of everything that God wants from us, what is at the top of his list? The answer came back, without hesitation, crisp and clear:

> "'Love the Lord your God with all your heart and with all
> your soul and with all your mind.' This is the first and
> greatest commandment. And the second is like it: 'Love
> your neighbor as yourself.' All the Law and the Prophets
> hang on these two commandments" (Matthew 22:37-
> 40).

Love is of first importance! All else is secondary. Peter declares that "above all" we should have love (1 Peter 4:8). Paul says that even if we possess the great qualities of eloquence, prophecy, wisdom, faith, and if we sacrifice to the point of martyrdom—but lack love, we are "nothing" (1 Corinthians 13:1-3).

We may lavish upon our children the finest things and the most expensive and stylish clothes; we may take them on the most exciting vacations and send them to the most prestigious schools; but if we do not make them feel loved, it is all to no avail. How many children have all of these things, yet remain empty, angry, depressed and discontented, simply because they do not feel close to their parents?

If there is closeness and love between us and our kids, we have a place to stand and a place to start. They are connected to us. They *want* to please us. They long to be near us. We have won the greatest battle of all—the battle for their hearts. But if there are no bonds of love, we are relegated to a ceaseless battle of wills in which there can never be a true victor.

As parents then, what we want to *have*, and what we want to *give*—above *anything* else—is love. If we build our families on love, our kids will be strong. Children raised in homes that are saturated with love are rarely drawn away into cliques of worldly kids or pulled into lawless gangs; the last thing they desire is to be alienated from the families they cherish so dearly. Such families are literal bulwarks and fortresses against the temptations, traps and corrosive effects of the world, serving to prevent most serious problems from ever gaining a foothold.

Kids are born with the capacity to love, but not all learn how. What can we do to get love into our children's lives?

1. Teach Them About God's Love

> "Jesus loves me! this I know, for the Bible tells me so;
> Little ones to him belong; They are weak but he is strong.
> Yes, Jesus loves me; Yes, Jesus loves me;
> Yes, Jesus loves me; The Bible tells me so."

These immortal words of Anna B. Warner have become the anthem of children all around the world. And so it should be. Little ones should be raised in an atmosphere saturated with God's love. They should be taught from infancy that God cares for them, knows all about them, takes delight in them, and longs to be close to them. Kids must grasp that God is a personal being who will be the closest friend they will ever have. *Your children's view of God is the most important lesson you will ever teach them.* It shapes their whole view of life and reality.

How many of us grew up with a negative view of God—a distant, dismal, impossible-to-please dictator whose frown of disapproval darkened the sunny days of our childhood? Some of us have spent years unlearning the intellectual and emotional view we at one time had of God.

I beg you, don't foist your miseries upon your children! Teach them of the great God of the Bible, the God who made them, sees them, longs to be their Father, and desires to be with them in heaven forever. Teach them of the God who is their shepherd, who knows them by name, who watches over them all the time, and who has assigned them their personal angel! (Matthew 18:10). They need to see that God is like Jesus, and that Jesus loved children and always took time to be with them.

89

2. Love Your Children

But don't all parents love their children? The answer, regrettably, is no. For some, children are a burden. An imposition. An accident. A society that can kill the unborn can fail to love the living. And some of us who would never dream of taking the lives of the unborn have killed the living by withholding our love from our own little ones who so desperately need it.

Parents who treat children as if they were a burden to be borne are not showing love. Many children who are giving their parents problems simply *do not feel loved.* We can yell, scream, rant, rave, beg, plead and punish, but until we change this feeling in their hearts, we won't ever get to first base! And let's be honest—some of us don't really love our children that much, anyway. We actually resent them, or we are just so consumed with our own needs and lives that our kids are just an unfortunate imposition. Maybe we loved them as infants, but they grew up and stopped being cute. (Have you ever had a child you just didn't *like* too much? It's probably the one who is most like you.) Remember, our children did not *ask* to be born into our families. We must give them the love God has freely given us!

To those who are failing to love our children I say, repent before you ruin your children, wreck your life, and lose *your* chance of going to heaven. God holds the strong under a higher accountability than the weak. If we have been given children to raise, this is a privilege and a sacred trust. God will hold us accountable for its faithful discharge. Some of us need to hear these sobering, no, frightening words of Jesus:

> "And whoever welcomes a little child like this in my name welcomes me. But if anyone causes one of these little ones who believe in me to sin, it would be better for him to have a large millstone hung around his neck and to be drowned in the depths of the sea" (Matthew 18:5,6).

God is watching, and he will judge! I pray that if we are guilty of lovelessness, we will see it, be grieved by our hardness of heart, and change immediately, before it is too late.

But how can we love our children?

Love each one

Each of our children should be special to us. We cannot play favorites without suffering the consequences. That was the fatal error of Isaac and Rebekah (Genesis 25:28) and Jacob (Genesis 37:4). The results in their families were catastrophic. Whether the oldest, middle, or youngest, each child should feel they have their own unique place in our hearts. Yes, there will be some kids that are easier to like and easier to be with. But we must imitate God in his absolute, unconditional love.

Love with your time and attention

We should notice our children and be aware of them. Whatever their age, we need to be tuned in to their needs. We cannot be so distracted that we become insensitive to their problems. Some children demand attention; others don't seem to need as much. The first one must not drive us away or take up all our time, and we cannot neglect the second.

It just takes *time*. In many ways, kids look at the time we give them as the most direct expression of our love. If we do not set aside time to be with them exclusively, they will not feel loved. If we find ourselves always saying, "Not now, I'm busy," then we are *too* busy! If we do not take the time *now*, we will try later, but it will be too late to catch up!

The love and attention that Jesus gave to children during his busy ministry tells us the kind of priority that we should give to our kids. On the occasion when his disciples sought to block the intrusion of little ones into his presence, Jesus became indignant.

91

He publicly rebuked his misguided followers and stopped what he was doing to spend time with the kids.

> People were bringing little children to Jesus to have him touch them, but the disciples rebuked them. When Jesus saw this, he was indignant. He said to them, "Let the little children come to me, and do not hinder them, for the kingdom of God belongs to such as these" (Mark 10:13-14).

With this example of our Lord before us, as busy as he was, dare any of us say we are too busy for our children? Time can be spent in longer stretches, such as going for a walk, playing or reading, but it can also be spent by taking a moment to pause and give a few precious minutes of total attention. We are wise when we take our children with us as we go out to run errands—we get two things done at once. Mostly, what they want and need, in any form they can have it, is some *exclusive* time spent with Mom and Dad. Such time says "I love you" in ways nothing else can.

Love with your touch

> "I tell you the truth, anyone who will not receive the kingdom of God like a little child will never enter it." And he took the children in his arms, put his hands on them and blessed them" (Mark 10:15-16).

I am sure Jesus could have blessed the children from afar; he could have smiled and waved as his limo rolled by. But antiseptic, impersonal "contact" was not his way; his was the way of closeness and affection.

We all need to be touched. There is nothing like the magic of human contact. Touch expresses what words and deeds cannot. God made us to need affection. We dry up emotionally without it. Read through the Gospels and note each time Jesus touched or was touched by someone. Touch is the language of love and intimacy. It breaks down barriers and says to people, "I love you. We are close. You have nothing to fear."

Unaffectionate families are cool, aloof and distant. They are not fun. There is an iciness and a reserve that is stifling, stuffy and sour. Children raised in such an atmosphere of distance develop a hard, nasty edge of anger and meanness. They are more prone to be disobedient, obstinate and to feel distant from parents. They are also more likely to have sexual hang-ups and marriage difficulties.

Some of us were raised in families that were unaffectionate. Perhaps there was love, but it was rarely expressed in direct or outward form. If so, we must realize that God does not want things that way in our homes now. Throughout the Scriptures, physical affection is modeled and enjoined: The father and son embraced and kissed in the parable of the prodigal son (Luke 15:20); God commands us to greet one another in the church with a holy kiss (Romans 16:16, 1 Corinthians 16:20); Paul and the church leaders in Ephesus embraced and kissed (Acts 20:37). God wants there to be generous expression of affection in his church and in our homes as well!

I remember coming to church the first time and seeing all the hugging. I was not from a background where physical affection was very prominent. It blew my mind! I at first thought there must be something wrong here. But then I realized that I was the one with the limited view of love. I began to change, and it produced a wonderful transformation in all my relationships, especially with those closest to me. Now, I touch my wife and children frequently. I have found that as my kids have gotten older they still need hugs, pats on the back, kisses on the cheek—actions that clearly say, "I love you."

If we as parents feel inadequate in this area, we just need to learn! We need to break down our pride, our inhibitions, our fears, our starchiness, and give our kids the love they crave. Strive to be more affectionate at home. It will be oil in the hard machinery of life!

Love with your expressions

By this I mean the expressions on our faces (our smile, our eyes) and our tone of voice. Children notice and read these things like a book. Harsh words and surly frowns do not give our kids a good feeling. Smile often at your children. This may seem like an obvious thing but note this week—how often do you look your child in the eyes and smile approvingly?

My wife Geri is a master (excuse me, mistress) of the beautiful voice, warm smile and sparkling eyes. When we are with others, I can barely get anyone to look my way. I have often found myself leaning my head at some ridiculous angle towards my wife so I will be noticed! I finally figured out that it wasn't because Geri is so beautiful (which she most certainly is) or because I am so ugly (no comment), but because of the smiling attentiveness she gives. Her voice is almost musical with a positive "up" tone about it. She laughs frequently, even at my lousy jokes. Her aura of warmth, joy and cheerfulness brightens and energizes our house and makes even difficult days more pleasant. Kids love to live in a family like this!

Love with your words

When David was about two years old, he began to come up to me and say, "I love you *too* Daddy!" I appreciated this, but it puzzled me. Was senility already upon me, in my early thirties? Was I going around saying "I love you" to my son and not remembering five seconds later?

I then realized that David had learned to say he loved me because of all the times he had heard me say it to him first. Therefore, his way of expressing it always came out as a response.

Do you get the point? Saying the words "I love you" teaches our children to love! They are born as a blank slate. They have the *capacity* to love but must be taught *how* by being shown and specifically by being *told* they are loved.

We just can't overdo it here. Kids need to hear the words "I love you" spoken sincerely and frequently by *both* parents! We also need to tell them what it is we love and like about them—what makes them special. Express love during those special times: bedtime, leaving for and returning from school and anytime you sense a hurt or fear. Of what are the lasting memories of childhood made? Not the expensive things and experiences we provide for them, but from the "little moments" of being happy and close.

3. Teach them to love others

As they have been loved, so they should love! Kids who are showered with love must be taught to give it away. If we do not teach our children to love, they will become selfish, aloof and arrogant. God loves us, but he *commands* us to love him in return and to love others as we love ourselves. Parents, we must imitate God's fatherly love in the way we *expect* our children to love us, love their siblings, and love those outside the family. Love is more than a natural response to being loved—it is a deliberate decision a child makes in response to the teaching and expectations of parents.

Love and concern for others should be talked about constantly, encouraged and praised. Teach them expressions of love such as saying "Hi" when people speak to them. It is rude to ignore or shrug away the greetings of other people. Teach them to look at people when they speak. Children learn to love by helping. They are capable of so much more than we think. Sometimes it seems the most conscientious parents have the lowest expectations for their children! We do far too much for them and in fact, create self-centeredness. Teach them to be sensitive and cooperative in meeting each other's needs in the family, especially watching out for their younger brothers and sisters. In our family we have worked long and hard on this one. We have had "servant's week" when everyone tried to "outdo one another in service." We have given stickers and made up charts to establish happy, helpful habits. Our emphasis is that the way we treat one another is actually the way we are treating Jesus himself (Matthew 25:34-40).

Children must come to understand that the whole family is an instrument of God to serve and reach out to other people. Loving, obedient children of Christian parents are one of the brightest lights that God will use in a dark and lost world! Encourage them to invite friends, teachers and acquaintances to church and to pray for specific people to become Christians. Get them involved! Let them experience the power of God at work through their lives and their prayers! They can learn very early to be "people lovers" with the great purpose of seeking and saving the lost, and helping the needy.

Our oldest son David was very shy and withdrawn in his early years. He seemed not to need people and could drift away into his own little world. Geri and I decided that this behavior was unacceptable and that we would do our best to teach David to be friendly, to care about others, and to "connect" with people. We urged him to look at people's faces when they spoke to him, smile and say, "Hi." Among family and close friends we gave him lots of affection and urged him to be warm and expressive. We shared repeatedly with him the biblical principles like "freely you have received, now freely give" and "give and it shall be given to you." All of this was done positively, firmly and consistently without making him feel self-conscious. We firmly believed he could be, in his own special way, a giving, warm, friendly child.

The application of God's principles worked beautifully! David is now an outgoing, confident young man who relates easily with people. His sensitivity is still there, but is now directed toward the feelings and concerns of others and not just himself. He was elected student body president of his elementary school, and two years running was the only player unanimously voted to the all-star squad by his soccer teammates. The other coaches and I believe that those votes came primarily because of his leadership and concern for his teammates.

David could have grown up as a socially withdrawn introvert who lived far beneath his potential. Instead, because of being given love and being taught how to love, he has matured to become a joyful, confident young man.

The Second Essential: Respect

"Honor your father and mother"—which is the first commandment with a promise—"that it may go well with you and that you may enjoy long life on the earth" (Ephesians 6:2-3).

The issue of respect for authority in the lives of children is absolutely critical. I am appalled at the arrogant, haughty, cocky attitudes I see in some children. They do not respect God, their parents, their teachers, adults, their baby sitters or other children. This is a devastating trend in our society and we must confront it in our churches as well. If we do not address and overcome this problem when we see it in our churches and homes, we will suffer a frightful loss of our kids to the world.

Many of us are blind to the fact that our children are arrogant and disrespectful. I am shocked at the attitudes and behaviors that many parents allow to go unchecked in their children. And I am not just talking about people out in the world, I am talking about Christians—disciples who ought to know better. Maybe we think it's cute, or maybe we think that this is the way all children are. I am afraid that some of us, in an attempt to make our kids into confident, strong, leader-types, have bred into our children an attitude of conceit and cockiness. We will live to reap the bitter harvest of our folly! Pride is not the necessary accompaniment of confidence and leadership. We must realize that pride is repugnant and offensive to God at any level, at any age, and that it must be rooted out.

How can we tell if our children are disrespectful? In younger children, it will come out with sassy talk, defiant looks, temper tantrums, stomping feet and hitting at you. With older kids it can be all the above, plus slamming doors, rolling eyes and muttering. The list is endless, and I'm sure many of us can add more to it!

Our position of honor and authority as parents is given to us by God. Our authority does not come because we are perfect— it is because God in his wisdom has arranged it this way. For our children to honor us is to show honor to God and his plan. As our children come to respect our authority, they learn to respect God himself; and then one day, when they are old enough, they will give God the ultimate honor of committing their whole lives to him. Therefore, parents, claim your authority! Expect to be respected! If you do not expect it, you will not get it!

Sometimes, we as parents lack confidence in dealing with kids. We feel guilty and inadequate. We become tentative. We suggest, plead, argue, wheedle and cajole. Our children sense our self-doubt, and they become more and more defiant. They also become less secure because what they really want down inside is the confidence that comes from knowing their limits. They want us to put up a fence around them—a fence that tells them just how far they can go. We need to put up the fence and tell the kids exactly where it is. They will try to run through it to see if it is real. Let them hit it a few times. They will soon learn that the fence is immovable but that within it they have total freedom and security. Then you will have respect!

The Third Essential: Obedience

Obedience to parents is the next of the four major areas of training that will produce godly character in our children. Obedience must be taught and expected early. It lays the foundation for obedience to all other authorities in life and ultimately to God.

Children who are rebellious, defiant and disobedient to parents later will demonstrate those same attitudes and behaviors toward all other authorities, be they teachers, babysitters, grandparents, employers, church leaders or law enforcement personnel.

By the time children are 18 months old, they usually are able to understand most of what is said to them, even though they cannot verbally communicate well. This is when early training of "Come here" and "Don't touch that!" begins. These are not games where they tease us by running away or touching whatever has been set off limits. When we give commands to our children, we speak as the God-ordained adult authority in their lives, and we must patiently, yet firmly expect obedience! How much easier it is to teach children to obey while they are young than to begin years later when the habit of disobedience is deeply established in their lives! Some of us have personally experienced the pain and devastation of living uncontrolled, disobedient lives. How difficult it was to learn "too late!"

Obedience is such a vital area that we will devote our next chapter entirely to this subject.

The Fourth Essential: Honesty

In order to have a relationship with God, we must love the truth, accept the truth, live by the truth and tell the truth. "You will know the truth, and the truth will set you free" (John 8:32). "...They perish because they refused to love the truth and be saved" (2 Thessalonians 2:10). Acceptance of the truth *for the love of truth alone* is the first and most important building block of character. Telling the truth to ourselves and to others enables us to be free and to have genuine relationships.

Parents, we must teach our children to accept, love and tell the truth. If they learn to accept the truth as children, they will be able to face their sins, repent of them, and be saved when they are older. If they always tell us the truth, no matter how difficult it is, we will be able to help them build a life based on righteous-ness.

Satan is a liar and the father of lies (John 8:44). When our children lie, we must realize they are taking a fateful step that can eventually wreck their lives. We must have deep convictions about this, or we will dismiss our children's deceit as a childish immaturity rather than treat it as a serious character issue. (I am speaking here of deliberate deceit and not harmless childish imagination.) We must catch it the first time it happens, and deal with it swiftly and powerfully.

We should not be continually fighting a battle to get our children to tell the truth. We should not ever have to wonder if we have the whole story. If we do not trust our kids' word, we have a serious problem that must be solved at all costs.

We confronted the lying issue with each of our children at age three. I don't know why, but that's just when they all told their first one.

One day, some college students were over at our house. We were outside in the front yard when one of them, Reese Neyland, walked over to me and said, "Elizabeth is coloring all over the front steps. I asked her about it and she said you gave her permission to do it." I went over, took a look, and sure enough, Elizabeth was happily coloring away literally *on* the steps. I said, "Elizabeth what are you doing?" She looked at me, then at Reese, and dissolved into a pool of tears. I knelt down, looked her in the eyes, and said, "Did you *lie* to Reese and say I gave you permission to do this?" She wailed "Yesssssss!" I reacted very strongly and told her that coloring on the steps was bad, but lying to Reese was even worse. She could tell by the depth of my indignation, shock, surprise and disappointment that this was just about the worst thing she had ever done. I don't remember all the disciplinary action we took, but it was strong. Geri and I both talked to her about it, read her the Scriptures, told her to make things right with God, with Reese and with us. She took it all very much to heart. Many years have passed since the coloring on the steps incident, but *none* of us involved has ever forgotten it. And best of all, Elizabeth, since that time, has never lied to us again.

With my son David, it was a bit different. He, at age three, began to "not remember" when we would ask him things. To some degree, he was right. David was (and is) so intense that he didn't hear anything unless we had a radar-lock on his eyeballs. But we began to notice increasing incidences of "I don't remember" or "I'm not sure" excuses when he got into trouble. It all came to a head one evening with the famous "Magic Pillows" caper.

David was playing in the family room. He had pulled all the pillows off the couch and onto the floor. I went in and told him that Mom did not want the pillows on the floor, so we put them back up on the couch. David stayed in the family room, and I got busy elsewhere around the house. Within a few minutes I had to go back into the now-empty family room, and I saw the pillows on the floor. I called David in and asked him if he did the deed. He got a panicky, puzzled look on his face and said, "I can't remember, I don't know." I checked with everyone else in the house and learned that no one else had even been in the room during those few minutes. David had to have been the one who did it, since he was the only person who had even been in the room.

But he still could not remember! It was part fear, part not paying attention to his actions, part mental block, and part self-protection; but I felt it was time for David's memory to function normally. I knew I could not back off—it was time to bring it to a head. David got into such a state of mental lockup that I think he *did* have trouble remembering whether he did or not. I explained to him he was the only one who *could* have done it, unless the pillows were "magic pillows" that in Disney-esque fashion could bounce themselves off the couch! I decided he could not eat with the family until he remembered. He needed time to think. He had to go to his room and search his memory banks. It was a lesson he had to learn, or he could conveniently forget anything he wanted, anytime it served his purpose. Things got a little intense there, but finally, David came and told me, "Dad, I think I do remember pulling those pillows off the couch. I am sorry." It was genuine. He had tried with all his might and got himself as far as he could. I accepted his apology. David's memory has improved remarkably since then! He has learned to be honest with himself, to face the truth, and to not give in to freezing up in panic when he is confronted with something unpleasant.

I tell these stories not to embarrass my children, but to illustrate the importance of taking a stand for truthfulness and to show the different ways children can skirt the truth. Accepting the truth, living by it, and not shading it in any way are qualities of character that you must model, teach and unflinchingly expect from your young ones. There are many other forms of dishonesty that you may face in raising a child. Don't be naive; learn to spot them. Deal with the problem in terms they understand, and you will find you can build honesty in your child's innermost character.

> Truthful lips endure forever, but a lying tongue lasts only a moment (Proverbs 12:19).

❦

You now know "The Four Essentials." Go back over this chapter, study the reference scriptures, and come to conviction about what you need to do. Talk with your spouse, and with your children, and go to work on things right away. If you do not give up, you will see the changes God wants in your family!

CHAPTER **6**

Winning Obedience
from Children

*Discipline your son, and he will give you peace; he will
bring delight to your soul (Proverbs 29:17).*

W E NOW COME TO THE NUTS AND BOLTS OF THE REAL LIFE RAISING
of children. How can we obtain quick and cheerful
obedience? How can we train in those qualities of
character and habits of conduct that will cause our
children to grow up to be a joy to us?

From the very beginning, children should learn to obey.
Obedience should be a habit, a pattern. It must not be a daily
battle we fight that makes our lives and theirs miserable. When
obedience is a habit, our families are happy. The arguing, yelling
and tension that most people consider a necessary evil simply will
not exist in our homes. We will have control. Our will and word

will be supreme. But we must believe that it should be and can be this way, or we will never see it happen!

The first principle of obedience we teach in our home is "first-time obedience." The kids know that they are to do what they are told immediately. We do not expect to have to tell them again. Children learn quite early just how far they can push us (or any authority) until action will be taken. Parents, we fall into a terrible trap when we find ourselves repeating our requests over and over, in a louder, more urgent tone, until our words are finally heeded. This is not true obedience! It sets a tone of nagging and arguing that ruins the atmosphere of a home. If this continues, we will find ourselves becoming increasingly weary and frustrated. We can even begin to dislike and resent our kids.

We have established this principle of first-time obedience by teaching it in family devotionals and by reinforcing it in passing conversations. We have fun ways of reminding everyone when we find ourselves slipping away from this: "When do we obey?" Mom or Dad asks. "The first time!," reply the kids.

Our second principle of obedience is "parents never lose." Geri and I decided a long time ago that we would not and could not lose any battle of obedience with our children if we were going to be effective parents. If you are ever defeated one time by a child they will be encouraged to challenge you again and again. *Never lose!* We have changed our minds when we realized we were unreasonable or mistaken, but we have informed the kids of this at the time so as not to confuse them. We have apologized when we felt it was warranted. But we have never just given up or given in, thus losing a battle of wills.

Sometimes the whole issue with a child comes down to one turning point, the epic "mother of all battles" upon whose outcome your future hangs. Such a struggle took place in our family with our son David when he was about two.

We were headed to my mother's home for a visit, about a two-and-a-half hour drive. David was strapped safely in the rear of the car in his car seat. He was well-fed, freshly changed and had plenty of toys with which to play—all set for a nice ride.

He didn't see it that way. He wanted to come up front and sit in his mom's lap. He started crying. Geri checked him again carefully to see if he was comfortable. He checked out fine. He just didn't like his seating assignment. He got louder. We tried to get him quiet—we sang songs, gave him toys, offered food, all to no avail. It was clear that this young man would be satisfied by one thing and one thing only—to come up front and sit on his mother's lap.

The way I viewed it, there were two good reasons for taking a stand: (1) It would be very unsafe for him to travel that way, and (2) it now had become a matter of principle.

We stopped looking back and drove on. David cried for almost two hours. It was not a fun trip. He finally fell asleep, exhausted, about 20 minutes away from my mother's house. We had won.

Someone might say, "Why didn't you just have his mother sit in the back with him?" My answer: to do so would have been a compromise that would have led to more compromises, and that would have changed forever the way our family traveled. Someone else might say, "Why didn't you spank him and have done with it?" My answer: I instinctively knew that this was a battle of wills that would have to be fought sooner or later and that we needed to exhaust his willpower rather than punish him. In retrospect, it proved to be exactly the right thing to do. We never again fought a single battle with David over his being put in the car seat, and he learned that he could not wear us down.

Compromise is one of the most devastating mistakes parents can make, and I have seen far too many people make it. It is as if our words mean *nothing*. We say something and we are argued with or ignored. We accept this as "normal" with kids. Absolutely not! It is normal because we let it be. When we do this, we sow the seeds of rebellion and exasperation (Ephesians 6:4) into our child's heart by our weakness. He or she will grow up to experience the infinitely harder disciplines of life, the law and God himself if we do not turn this around.

If you have been failing here, sit down with your children, get out the Bible, and read them the passages about obeying. Talk to them about how God has given you the responsibility to raise them and how they have the responsibility to obey. Talk to them about obeying "the first time." Tell them that it has not been that way, and that you, and they, are going to change. Obtain their agreement, have a prayer together, and from that time on, be different. Don't give up until the habit of obedience is permanently established in your home!

Recognizing Disobedience

Half the battle is recognizing when our kids are disobedient. Let's look at four different types of disobedient behavior:

Defiant disobedience

This is fairly easy to spot, even for the wimpiest, most deluded parent. It starts out with "No!" and is often accompanied by a stomping foot and a curled lip. We are shocked and intimidated by such brashness and either give in quickly or wear down over time. Sometimes we debate it with them (have you ever found yourself down on the floor arguing with a three-year-old?), or we excuse it by saying, "Well, you're just tired." The fact, plain and simple, is that you have been beaten. You lack willpower! You are a fearful parent, and you will pay for your compromising ways by raising an insecure, defiant, spoiled brat.

Our oldest daughter Elizabeth is now a confident, assertive, respectful young woman. But in her early years, she was incredibly strong-willed and defiant. Things got so bad that on one occasion I found myself searching the Yellow Pages, looking in vain for "Exorcist: We make house calls."

Elizabeth took on Geri and decided she would make a run at being "Head Woman" in our house. Often, I would come home and hear Elizabeth's cries from behind her closed door, and find Geri muttering repeatedly, "I'm going to win, I'm going to win." And win she did! Geri and I together broke Elizabeth's defiance without crushing her spirit. To do this, we had to be lovingly firm and we could never let her wear us down. At around five years, Elizabeth settled down and became a delight, but that was because she knew she could never defeat us, and that it was in her best interest to obey.

Her next big struggle took place at 14 years old when Elizabeth had to wrestle with her decision to become a disciple. She came through in great shape! But we are convinced to this day that if we had allowed her to conquer us in her early years, she would not be who she has become today.

Disarming disobedience

Have you ever had a kid who could crack you up laughing while he or she was disobeying you? This little manipulator can smile at us, do something funny and melt us right on the spot. We try to justify ourselves by repeating those fateful words: "But he (or she) is so *cute!*" But the fact is, we lost!

If we let a child control us by smiling and laughing, we will cry and mourn later! We are creating a monster who will learn to maneuver his or her way through life, manipulating others for personal gain.

Our son Jonathan is a card. He has a dry sense of humor that gets everyone laughing. He does imitations, tells jokes, the whole bit. He began to wear glasses early on, and with the overalls and suspenders that he always wore, he looked like a cute, innocent "little professor."

I was taken in a bit, but Geri spotted the strong will beneath the charm. "Just cross him," she said, "and you'll see what's inside". She was right. Inside the smile was a stubborn will and a very bad temper that came out if he did not get his way. We learned to enjoy Jonathan, and to laugh with him and at him, but to never let him do whatever he wished just because he was so charming.

Deaf disobedience

Some kids act as if we don't exist. Words have no impact on them. We tell them to do something, and we get back silence or an unintelligible grunt, but no action. We repeat our request, but get the same results. We might even get verbal agreement, *but nothing ever happens* ! This, too, is disobedience! It is passive, and it often goes undetected, but it is wrong!

There should not have to be a *single* repetition, much less continual repetition. If this is not your expectation and pattern, your kids will learn to be lazy and slow to obey. They also will learn that you eventually will give up, do it yourself, or forget about it. If you allow this to go unchecked, it ultimately will destroy a child's character, and it will wear you out as well.

Our son David was so adept at deaf disobedience that we had his ears checked for bad hearing. We did this several times, and he tested out fine. I finally came to suspect it was an attitude problem and not a hearing problem. I conducted my own experiment to prove my theory. One afternoon when David was out riding his Big Wheel, I called him in for dinner. It seemed as if he did not hear me, so I called louder. No response. I walked to the curb and called again—not even a flicker of response. Finally, I jumped in his path, grabbed the steering wheel, leaned down and said again, "David, come to dinner NOW!" That's what it took to get his attention.

The next day, I ran another test—similar weather conditions, same Big Wheel, same time of day. Standing at a great distance from the road, I said in hushed tones to Geri, "Why don't we take the kids to get ice cream?" VROOM! Dust swirled; rocks flew everywhere. The smoking tires of the Big Wheel were suddenly dangerously close to my toes. David, his eyes glittering with expectation, looked up at me and said, "Ice cream? Are we going to get ice cream?" I knew from that moment on, David could hear just fine, he had been hearing only what he *wanted* to hear. We worked with him, taught him to listen, and things improved greatly.

If you have a kid who is not listening to you, you must realize how serious it is. I would suggest that you study the Book of Proverbs to deepen your own convictions. Then, sit down, and study those same verses with your children and teach them to give you their attentive, respectful obedience.

Dreary disobedience

This may be the most exasperating and effective resistance to your authority that a child can display. It is utilized by all children to some degree and by some children with deadly effect. I am talking about the tearful, self-pitying, poor-me act that can drive parents into fits of guilt, rage and frustration. This child does not refuse to obey, but puts up a barrage of moaning and complaining. We either come to believe we are the meanest slave-driver parents who ever lived, or we just get tired of hearing all the whining and give in.

We fail to recognize this behavior for what it is—a form of disobedience. We write if off as "kids being kids" because it seems that all kids do it. We accept our children's outward conformity to our wishes, even though it is accompanied by grumbling, fussing and tears. To do so is to accept actions done with the wrong attitudes! You must realize that this is a character flaw that will one day produce an unhappy, self-pitying adult.

God condemns grumbling and complaining in the Scriptures:

> Do everything without complaining or arguing, so that you
> may become blameless and pure, children of God without
> fault in a crooked and depraved generation, in which you
> shine like stars in the universe as you hold out the word of
> life... (Philippians 2:14-16).

God does not accept grumbling, resentful obedience from his children. He wants a cheerful, loving acceptance of his will even when it is difficult. If this is what God expects of us, then it is also what we should expect of our children.

In our society, grumbling is pervasive. Whining is a national pastime. We accept it as a fact of life. Even though it makes life unpleasant, and even though the Lord forbids it, we put up with it. I am reminded of another group of spoiled children who grumbled—the children of Israel:

> The rabble with them began to crave other food, and again
> the Israelites started wailing and said, "If only we had meat
> to eat! We remember the food we ate in Egypt at no cost—
> also the cucumbers, melons, leeks, onions and garlic. But
> now we have lost our appetite; we never see anything but
> this manna!"...Moses heard the people of every family
> wailing, each at the entrance to his tent. The Lord became
> exceedingly angry, and Moses was troubled. (Numbers
> 11:4-6, 10)

We learn from other passages that any grumbling we do is really grumbling against God. Moses pointed this out when he said "Who are we? You are not grumbling against us, but the Lord" (Exodus 16:8b). God met the needs of the Israelites when they complained, but he also punished them for their attitude (Numbers 11:33).

As parents we must see that a fussing, whining spirit is offensive to God. It springs from selfishness and ingratitude of which we must repent. God wanted to know the needs of his children, and he did not mind them making them known. What he did not accept, and what we must not accept, is complaining. We must teach our kids to be grateful for what they have and not to feel that we and the rest of the world is there to cater to their every pleasure and preference. We must teach our kids to express their wishes, opinions, likes and dislikes, but in a pleasant, positive tone of voice.

In our family (which is rather large) there must be plenty of give and take on things like menus, seat occupancy, recreational decisions and the like. We have taught the kids how to express their wishes and present their point of view without whining and to accept the final decision with a positive attitude. We have taught them the proper voice tone over and over until it has come out right. It takes determination and unceasing proactive teaching, but the establishment of a positive spirit in children is worth any effort!

The Power of Discipline

What are we to do when our children disobey us? How do we react? What options are open to us? In what follows I provide seven suggestions. Realize that what works in one situation may not work in another and that what is effective with one child may not be effective with another. Use wisdom and trial and error to help you discover what gets the best results.

Verbal correction or reprimand

This is the simplest and most common of all corrective disciplines. It involves the most basic of instructions: "Come here." "Not that way, this way." "Don't do that." "Don't say that."

One-warning rule

If your instructions are not followed, give one verbal warning. If you still are not heeded, then more serious consequences ensue. This principle should be taught to your children, clearly explained to them, and continually reinforced. Once laid out, it should be adhered to unflinchingly.

Immediate correction

The closer to the time of the offense, the more effective the action. If you wait, kids have time to forget, distort or rationalize. Delay also creates a tense, fearful atmosphere.

Temporary isolation

This works great with kids who love to be in the middle of the action. Putting them in a corner, into a neutral (boring) room or into their own room can be extremely effective. It prevents them from ruining everyone else's fun with their disobedience. Never let a grumbling, complaining child bring down the whole family's mood. This is actually one way they learn to gain control over us--we simply don't want the disruption, so we let them have their way. Don't give in! Outsmart them by sending them away with the words, "We're all going to be having a great time out here, and when you get a happy attitude you can come out and join the fun!" They fret and fuss all alone until they conclude, "No one out there seems to be mourning the loss of my wonderful presence. As a matter of fact, everybody but me is having a blast. I guess I better get my attitude right." But remember, they do not come out until there has been a *complete* change of heart.

Temporary loss of possessions or privileges

Another way to stay one step ahead of your kids is to deprive them of a special possession or privilege. We have found this to be especially effective if it is reserved for the more serious offenses. It can work with any age and actually becomes more effective as children grow older. Consider what they love to do or enjoy playing with. Take some time, talk about it with your spouse, and come up with a deprivation of activity or possessions that will help them deal with their misdeeds.

As a youngster of two, David loved his Big Wheel. I don't remember what the horrible crime was, but we said, "You can't ride your Big Wheel for two days." We soon found him sitting stationary upon it, experiencing a voyeuristic fulfillment in spite of our punishment. We said, "You can't even sit on it." Then we found him *standing* next to it with a hand on the steering wheel, once again getting a "Big Wheel fix." We went one more step: "David, you can't even *touch* it." That did it! Now he felt the loss. He stood there in the garage with a faraway look in his eyes, remembering days of glory on his Big Wheel and vowing to never again repeat his crime. It worked so well that this was the only time in his young life that we ever had to take this drastic measure.

Elizabeth, at age three, committed a major offense.

"No cookies, honey, for two days."

"But what about juice and cookies time at preschool?" she protested.

"No, not even there. We will talk to your teachers. You can have the celery and carrots (yum!), but no cookies."

It proved to be very effective. Why? Because for two days she had to remember and see a consequence for her actions. In this case, it worked better than anything else we could have done.

You will find that this type of action, wisely and judiciously taken, is more effective as children move into the middle school and teen years. Parties, sports leagues, telephone, special trips—all these are privileges that can be taken away temporarily to teach a lesson or reinforce an attitude.

The most important aspect of this is to think clearly through it and get help from your spouse before you open your mouth. This discipline should be used wisely and be reserved for serious issues. Don't take things away for every offense—this diminishes impact and creates exasperation. Don't react in anger. How many of us, in the heat of battle, have dictated some foolish punishment, such as, "You are grounded for six months!" only to realize later that the punishment was overkill, unenforceable, or would end up hurting the whole family?

Extra work or jobs to do

Some kids don't mind correction or spankings as long as they get away with whatever they did. To counter this, give extra work. If it relates to the disobedience in some way, it is even more effective. Cleaning up the mess they made, taking an extra turn on the dishes, washing the car, working to pay off something carelessly broken—all of these create a deeper sense of responsibility. The punishment is actually a form of restitution.

Spanking

What does the Bible say? Is it right or wrong? Consider these verses:

> He who spares the rod hates his son, but he who loves him is careful to discipline him. (Proverbs 13:24).

> Folly is bound up in the heart of a child, but the rod of discipline will drive it far from him (Proverbs 22:15).

> Do not withhold discipline from a child; if you punish him with the rod, he will not die. Punish him with the rod and save his soul from death (Proverbs 23:13-14).

The message is clear: Spanking is a valid, recommended and healthy form of discipline. When employed with wisdom and love, it works powerfully. It is virtually irreplaceable in the early years. Since spanking can be abused and because there is so much legitimate concern today about inappropriate physical punishment, let me give some guidelines on this widely misunderstood subject.

1. A spanking should be an event. We should draw children aside to a private location before spanking them. A spanking is *not* a "pop" or "whop" out of the blue as we pass by a child we see doing something wrong. Such actions on our part are not only ineffective, but wrong!

2. Explain beforehand the reason for the spanking. Grabbing a child, paddling them, and trying to explain in the midst of the punishment, or afterwards, does no good and is unfair. Not explaining at all is even worse. How can something be effective when the reasons are unstated or unclear? A child should understand the exact reason for the spanking before it is given.

3. Cool off before spanking a child. When we are overly emotional or in a rage, we *must* wait until we have complete self-control before administering a spanking. When our passions are aroused, we can do and say things that are absolutely wrong. A spanking is a righteous and just discipline, not a retaliatory, frustrated outburst. Screaming, cursing and terrorizing a child is sinful!

4. Use a designated paddle or some flat object as the "rod." The "rod" gives the whole event a judicial air rather than a feeling of personal attack. It is best to decide in advance what to use, so that we don't grab some unsafe implement in the heat of the moment. There are different schools of thought on the definition of the term "rod." Some people believe that it must be a flexible "switch," others feel the term is not so specific. (Geri and I have used a small, flat paddle.) The primary issue is that whatever you use must be weighty enough to get the job done and light enough to inflict no

damage or injury. We should never use our hand to spank with the possible exception of the light slap on the wrist given to the very young children in the earliest days of discipline. The hand is ineffective with older children and is too personal.

5. Spank on the "safe" backside or thigh. Spankings delivered to these places sting, but do not injure. A spanking should be firm enough to bring tears, but not so hard as to cause bruises or welts. *Never* strike a child on the face—this is simply too degrading and humiliating. Never strike them on any part of the body where they could be injured. Never should we strike a child with our fists or kick them, push them, slam them into a wall, or throw them to the ground. This is abuse, not discipline. Jerking a child around by the hand or arm is disrespectful and dangerous.

6. Spankings must result in a changed, contrite heart. If there is no sorrow or change of attitude, we have only angered and embittered our child. Spankings must be strong enough, and applied wisely enough, to change the attitude.

7. Bring things to a resolution. The youngster should have a total understanding of what he or she did wrong and make a complete apology. We should then extend complete forgiveness. If this does not happen, we risk the creation of a sullen, brooding rebel. The air should be clear and our relationship completely restored when everything is over.

8. Do not spank for every offense. Spanking is not always called for, nor does it work as effectively on all children. Some kids are virtually oblivious to spankings, and others are totally crushed by them. Use another form of discipline if it works better. As children enter the elementary school years, spanking becomes increasingly less appropriate.

9. Start as soon as a child begins to understand the word "No." At approximately 14 months or so, our little ones begin to understand us. As soon as they do, they begin to assert their wills against ours! At first, we simply need to speak firmly to our children and then physically move them or the object that is the problem. There will come a time, though, when a light slap on the wrist along with a strong "no" is needed.

❦

In closing our thoughts on discipline, let me make three very important suggestions.

First, **be consistent.** Establish some basic rules and limits and stick to them. Do not allow moods or weariness to affect your standards. It is extremely frustrating to our children if we vary our position from day to day. Put up the "fence" and leave it there. To vacillate is to embitter and discourage! You lose their respect, and the children become increasingly sullen and defiant.

Second, parents must always **be unified** on disciplinary matters. Never argue in front of the kids about discipline. Work out mutually agreed standards in private, then back each other up. If the kids see that you are divided, it will create havoc beyond belief. They will play you against each other, and it can threaten the very life of your marriage. Talk things out. Come to unity. If need be, get responsible advice to help resolve disciplinary differences. Also, when you see that your spouse is frazzled, weary and irritable, step in and give him or her some help in dealing with the kids. It's a team effort and we must stay unified.

Most of you reading this book now realize that you are going to have to crack down and that there are going to have to be major changes. The problem for some of you is that your kids are older now and are not accustomed at all to the strong discipline they need. This brings us to the third thing we need to do: **Make a definite plan.** My suggestion is to have a family meeting, and using the appropriate scriptures, talk about God's plan for raising kids. Explain that you have not been doing it this way, but that you are under conviction that things must change. Go over a few of the changes that will need to be made, have a prayer, then get started! Don't tackle everything at once. Select your battles carefully. If you get too picky or try to change everything overnight, you will drive yourself and your kids crazy. Start with some basics, and build up from there.

When it comes to discipline many parents fall into one of two extremes. They either practice something much more akin to child abuse, or they go to the opposite end and neglect discipline altogether. I suggest that you reread this section several times and study carefully the scriptures that have been referenced. It is vital for your children that you properly understand your responsibility and wisely and lovingly provide the correction and discipline they so much need.

7

God's Training Plan

Train a child in the way he should go, and when he is old
he will not turn from it (Proverbs 22:6).

Principles

TRAINING IS DIFFERENT FROM DISCIPLINE. BY NATURE, IT IS
proactive, whereas discipline is reactive. With training
we *build*, with discipline we *alter*. Both are absolutely
essential. Attempting to raise kids by discipline alone,
without training, creates negativity and frustration. On the other
hand, training without discipline is foolhardy and weak and
underestimates the rebelliousness of human nature. As parents
we must become equally proficient in both areas.

To get a better view of the concept of training, let us examine
in depth the passage which best articulates this wonderful concept:

Hear, O Israel: The LORD our God, the LORD is one. Love
the LORD your God with all your heart and with all your

soul and with all your strength. These commandments that
I give you today are to be upon your hearts. Impress them
on your children. Talk about them when you sit at home and
when you walk along the road, when you lie down and
when you get up. Tie them as symbols on your hands and
bind them on your foreheads. Write them on the doorframes
of your houses and on your gates (Deuteronomy 6:4-9).

Let's break it down and discuss the key phrases:

"These commandments" (v.6)

The Bible is the undergirding basis of all training. It is the
very Word of God, to be revered, loved and believed by children.
It is the standard which has authority over us and them. It is a
wonderful thing to be taught the Bible from infancy. Some of us
act as if this is somehow a disadvantage. Far from it! Think of the
millions of young people that have been horribly scarred forever
because they were reared godlessly with no moral standard. Both
we and our children should consider it a priceless privilege, not
a detriment, to be raised in a home where the Bible is taught. Such
was the home of young Jesus, and of young Timothy, of whom
Paul said "from infancy you have known the holy Scriptures" (2
Timothy 3:15).

"Love the Lord your God" (v.5)

Training flows from a *relationship* of love with a personal God
(see Chapter 1). Training emphasizes a life that pleases God, not
simply conformity to a standard. If we teach our kids the Bible
with a "do-it-or-else" mentality, we have missed the point and
will live to see our children walk away from God. The Bible should
not be opened up only when we want some extra authority to
"straighten out" a child; instead, it should be used continually to

teach kids about who God is and about his great plan for their lives.

"These commandments...are to be upon your hearts" (v.6)

You must train at the heart level! The Word should be written "in their hearts and. . .on their minds" (Hebrews 10:16). Love God, love his word, get your kids to take it deeply into their hearts, and then they will *never* let it go!

"Impress them on your children" (v.7)

Training with the Scriptures must be done with great conviction, sincerity and earnestness. If you casually read off a few passages and talk about a few ideas, you will get nowhere! Kids know what is important to you. If you want your training to stick, you will have to give it all you've got.

"Talk about them when you sit at home...walk along the road...lie down...when you get up" (v.7)

Train constantly—anywhere, anytime, any place. It is meant to be a natural part of life. Training is not the dreaded "lecture" kids sit through and forget about as soon as it is over. It is not nagging our kids about their misdeeds. Training is the wonderful experience of teaching our children about life while we live it— that's what makes it fun, effective and doable. Some of us think of training as if it were a classroom lecture or a counseling appointment. If we confine it to this, we will never get the job done. The fact is, we just can't raise kids by appointment! Most of the teaching Geri and I do is spontaneous, occurring during the normal activities of life.

Such training makes spiritual things real and down to earth to children. If we lapse into a vocal "holy tone" when we decide to be "spiritual" and teach the kids about God, they will blow us off as religious phonies. If the only training they are getting is in a discipling time or at church classes, it will not be nearly enough.

We must never underestimate how many times we will have to say the same things over and over. Develop your own catchy sayings that you repeat continually in your family. Don't be discouraged! They are learning, even if at times it seems they are not. It is the nature of kids (and all of us) that the same things have to be taught repeatedly. As I have often said, "Life consists of learning the lessons you should have already learned."

Specifics

What are some things we train into our kids?

Character

All of us have a basic temperament. Start very early with your kids, building upon their good points and strengthening any areas of weakness. They should begin to learn who they are, the good and the bad, pretty soon in life. Teach them early on to "cleanse the inside of the cup" and not just put on an act. "Even a child is known by his actions, by whether his conduct is pure and righteous" (Proverbs 20:11).

Beliefs and faith in God

Trusting God in prayer, standing on the truth of God's promises, is an issue of training, as is going by the standard of the Bible in all areas of belief and practice.

Attitudes

Train a great, positive, "can-do" winning spirit into your children. Teach them to love life, to expect the best, to be glad that God made them just who they are. Teach them to expect God to work powerfully, and that there is never a reason to remain discouraged.

Values

Good morals, such as honesty, sexual purity and the avoidance of drugs should be taught and explained. Put in these values while the children are very young, and they will never abandon them.

Personality, demeanor and manners

Train them to have pleasant personality traits. If a child has a grating or offensive manner, don't let it just go on! Some of us need to realize that our kids really aren't that likable. Their personalities are offensive. If you spot this, deal with it; if others point it out to you, check it out, then take action. Don't let your kid grow up a social outcast because of a weird, quirky or rude personality. Some kids think they are hilarious when they are not; others act strange to get attention; some are bland wall flowers. Go to work on these kinds of things, being careful not to break their confidence.

Teach your offspring to have a pleasant countenance, to look directly at people in conversation and to have a fun, happy spirit. Don't let them be a negative sourpuss! Train in things such as politeness, table manners, hygiene and social graces. Crass, rude or wild youngsters who smart off, destroy other kids' possessions and create mayhem while visiting in other people's homes must be confronted and changed! That is your job as a parent—do not neglect it!

Work ethic and responsibility

Hard work and a sense of responsibility are habits of character that can be trained into a child. Laziness is a fatal flaw that forever will mire them in the morass of underachievement. Therefore, teach and inculcate an ethic of hard work.

Geri and I have used the book of Proverbs liberally on this great subject:

> A sluggard does not plow in season; so at harvest time he looks but finds nothing (Proverbs 20:4).

> The sluggard says, "There is a lion in the road, a fierce lion roaming the streets" (Proverbs 26:13).

> As a door turns on its hinges, so a sluggard turns on his bed (Proverbs 26:14).

We have stressed repeatedly with our children that they should "love hard work." And even if it is a struggle for them to be motivated, they realize what the goal is.

School work is a character issue. If you train your kids to work hard, be responsible and do their best, school will, in all likelihood, never be a problem. All you need to know is: Are they giving it their all? Are they working hard? If they are, the grades will usually take care of themselves. We have never made grades the huge issue that some parents do—that is the wrong focus. Instead, make diligence and excellence the issue. Challenge your kids to be disciplined, to pay attention in class, and to do their very best work. Then you can be proud of them, based on their effort. Usually, unless there is some other problem, the grades will be fine—probably well above average, since so many kids in their classes aren't trying very hard.

It helps immensely if you get your oldest child well-trained and highly motivated. The younger ones will more than likely follow suit. Elizabeth, our oldest, has always loved school, has loved to learn and has worked hard in her academics. She has excellent grades. Now, the others imitate Elizabeth's work ethic. Our oldest son David has made it his habit to come in and do his homework immediately after school. Now his younger brother Jonathan does the same thing. It is simply a matter of good training producing a good example which is then imitated by the next child.

Give appropriate jobs and responsibilities around the house. Early on, get the kids to make their beds, clean their rooms, and put up their things. Household chores such as setting the table, sweeping, folding clothes and doing dishes should be assigned fairly. A word of caution: Don't let your harder working kids do everything for the others. And don't *you* do everything for them either! Our kids all have their different jobs, and they tackle them with gusto. It is not a battle to get them to work. They have learned to enjoy the after-dinner clean up as a fun time. We give them allowances apportioned to age, the responsibilities they have and their faithfulness in carrying them out.

The Reward Concept

As I said earlier, training is a proactive, positive thing. It removes the need for continual discipline and correction by filling up a child's life with good. Use the concept of reward to build in positive traits. For younger ones, make charts so they can earn stars for good behavior and be rewarded by a prize after accumulating a certain amount. We have found that the stronger and more difficult the child, the greater the need for goals and rewards.

Geri discovered this with Elizabeth when she was very young. So many battles were being fought over attitude that Geri created a chart for her with the desired actions written down on the left and with a grid to the right. Every action was followed by the word "happily." It went like this: "Gets dressed happily;" "Goes to bed happily;" "Brushes teeth happily," etc. At the end was a picture of a long-desired, incredibly amazing lunch box that would be awarded after the accumulation of 50 stars. Elizabeth's behavior changed radically! It was a joy for us and for her. After much hard work, she proudly went to school with her brand new lunch box, and we fixed up a new chart!

The concept continues to work as children get older. Elizabeth is now a young woman, but she still does her very best when she has a clear, tangible goal for which to shoot. Parents, praise good behavior and reward it with increased freedom and privileges. In the end, you will have a child trained in character and life that will be a joy and a delight to you, even into old age.

> Buy the truth and do not sell it;
> Get wisdom, discipline, and understanding.
> The father of a righteous man has great joy;
> He who has a wise son delights in him.
> May your father and mother be glad;
> May she who gave you birth rejoice
> (Proverbs 23:23-25).

CHAPTER **8**

Nurturing Confidence in Children

For you have been my hope, O Sovereign Lord, my confidence since my youth (Psalm 71:5).

T AKE A TRIP BACK INTO YOUR CHILDHOOD AND REMEMBER SOME remark or incident that especially damaged your confidence. Do you recall the sense of self-disgust, shame and embarrassment that swept over you? Chances are, even as you remember it now, those very same emotions will cause your pulse to quicken and your face to blush. As parents we often forget the pain and difficulties we endured in our formative years as we sought to build some sort of identity and security.

One of my most embarrassing moments happened when I was in the eighth grade. (May God protect middle schoolers!) The county fair was in town, and I got up all my courage and asked the girl down the street out on my very first date. To my amazement, even though she was taller than I, she said "Yes"! I was excited beyond belief. After much agonizing, I decided on my outfit: blue jeans, white shirt, white socks, penny loafers and a sporty new corduroy red vest. (Let the reader understand: To wear the Red Vest was a declaration that one thought oneself worthy of the designation "cool." Since I was new to this school, I was hereby laying it all on the line.)

When the big day finally arrived, I was so nervous that my breath came in short, shallow gulps. My mother took us over to the fairgrounds and dropped us off. At first, everything went along nicely. We walked around, took in the sights, and tried to win some prizes—all the while ingesting generous amounts of popcorn and cotton candy. Then we hit the rides.

Now to say that I was susceptible to motion sickness is to vastly understate the case. As a matter of fact, I had been known to get queazy on Interstate exit ramps. I considered this fact for a moment, but felt somehow that my manhood was on the line, and so we sallied forth. It was to be the greatest mistake of my young life.

The Scrambler. . .made it! The Octopus (a much greater test) ...made it...sort of. I began to feel a little woozy. I should have known better than to challenge my system again, but folly drove me onward to inevitable disaster. It happened at the very apex of the normally harmless Double Ferris Wheel. The wheel stopped, the seat rocked back and forth, the world began spinning, and yes. . .I lost it. Regurgitated. Blew chunks. Tossed cookies. Called Ralph. Hurled. Spewed. Barfed. My seat belt prevented me from leaning over the side of the car. My whole outfit, including the once glorious Red Vest, was now an obscenity. The tattooed guy operating the ride looked up and took it all in with a fiendish, leering grin. He left us up there rocking as long as he could before bringing us down.

I was an absolutely disgusting, revolting mess. I had to stay in that condition for what seemed an eternity before my mother came to pick us up. My date was actually very kind and compassionate, but I was humiliated beyond description. What did she really think? What would happen to me at school when this got out?

I tell this story to remind us how tough it was "back then." From that first trip on the school bus right down to the last hurrah at the senior prom, early life is one long struggle for self-esteem! Kids can be viciously cruel to one another. They will label and ridicule any aberration; they will call names, exclude, bully and tease. If we are not watchful, we will be completely oblivious to the tremendous difficulties our children may be facing. Some of us need to wake up!

We cannot protect our kids entirely from the hard knocks of life, nor should we. What we can do, however, is give them the guidance and inner confidence that will enable them to over-come. As our children's primary mentors, we must help them develop both an unconceited confidence and a healthy humility. These are treacherous waters, and we will need wisdom and help from the Scriptures to navigate our way through them.

Wrong Foundations of Confidence

Let us first identify the false foundations, so that we might not build on a faulty foundation.

Physical appearance

From day one, we are judged and judge others, by appear-ance. According to the standards of a particular society, people are attractive, so-so or homely. Tall or short, fair or dark skin, straight hair or curly, petite or large. . .you fit in or you don't. Many kids spend huge amounts of mental energy trying to figure out if they look good, or bemoaning their supposed ugliness. For some children, coming to terms with their physical appearance is one of the great battles of life.

My wife has seen my old pictures from elementary school, and she says I was a cute kid. That is certainly not the way I felt about myself! I was too short and had big ears, red hair and freckles. I was sure that everybody else (with the possible exception of my mother) thought I looked really dumb. Only later in life, when I read my Bible and came to admire young David, who was short and had red hair, did I begin to think that maybe my appearance was okay.

Many parents have been taken in by the world's standards of judgment. We overvalue beauty. We make it a big deal. When we do so, we are setting up our children for problems. They will gauge their own self-worth by their appearance and will judge others that way as well. What happens when someone better looking comes along? What if they should ever suffer a disfiguring injury, and what happens as they get older?

To build confidence on a solid foundation, you first need to give God the credit for every gift your child has, including any gifts of appearance. Believe it yourself, and teach it to them continually. This gives a child assurance but also gives them a sense of humble appreciation. Second, teach them to value the inside above the outside as God does:

> But the Lord said to Samuel, "Do not consider his appearance or his height, for I have rejected him. The Lord does not look at the things man looks at. Man looks at the outward appearance, but the Lord looks at the heart" (1 Samuel 16:7).

Athletic prowess

Very quickly, kids notice who is faster, stronger and more coordinated. Such children are generally more popular and usually become leaders, especially among boys. Being athletic is a wonderful gift but is not a valid basis for the judgment of character. Consider some of the great athletes of our time whose personal lives are totally lacking in virtue. No, being gifted with speed, strength and agility is not the ultimate good in life! We have said in other places in this volume how important it is for children to develop physically, but they must not judge the worth of themselves or others on that basis.

Intelligence

"Aren't you smart!" we say about our bright little one, and very soon in school the evaluation of brain power is a daily occurrence. Being called "dumb" or "stupid" ranks a kid right at the bottom of the social ladder. The fact is all of us have known some awfully foolish smart people, and their high I.Q.'s only made them worse! Wisdom is the quality God admires, and it is a product of character, experience and obedience to God—qualities that are attainable for all.

Geri and I value good grades, but we appreciate great effort even more. If our children are giving their best, then we encourage and applaud them. We are aware of grades, and we reward them, but we believe it is a mistake to put the primary focus there.

Material possessions

The kid who has the coolest bike, hottest car, newest CD player, latest video game or the most up-to-date clothes has a leg up in our society. It is actually quite amazing how many "friends" possessions can attract. The TV ads preach the message: "You've got to have this to be cool"—and we literally buy into that way of thinking.

We let our backgrounds bias us. Some of us grew up rich, others poor. We are horrified that our kids aren't dressed in the most expensive clothes—like we were as children. Or, we are determined that they will have the very best of things that we never had.

How superficial and worldly this is, and how far from God's way! Jesus said: "'Watch out! Be on your guard against all kinds of greed; a man's life does not consist in the abundance of his possessions'" (Luke 12:15). Don't let your kids grow up thinking they are better or worse than others because of what they have or don't have. And remember: It is fine to be generous with your kids and let them dress fashionably, but they must not have their confidence in or their focus upon mere outward appearance.

Mistakes Parents Make

In addition to building on a wrong foundation, there are many other errors we can make that undermine our children's confidence. Listed below are nine of the most common:

Being basically critical

If you mostly see the negative things about your kids, then that is what they will see about themselves. If you think the best way to motivate them is by telling them they are no good and harping on their mistakes, you are dead wrong! This may be the way you were treated by your parents, but please do not repeat this sin with your kids! Everyone saw Simon son of John as an emotional, unstable hothead; Jesus saw him as a great leader and a man of faith and changed his name to Peter, the "Rock". And that is just what he became!

Failing to teach

Take the time to teach the basic things, from social skills to how to throw a ball. The results will amaze you! You also will reap the side benefit of becoming much closer to your kids.

Failing to express specific esteem, praise and admiration

A generalized expression of love is just not enough. We must say *what* we love, like, respect and appreciate about our kids in very understandable, concrete terms.

Spending little or no exclusive time

Kids form their self-esteem based upon the kind and amount of time we give them. If we are always "too busy," they will conclude that they are unimportant and worthless.

Failing to understand unique needs

Children, like adults, are motivated or discouraged in different ways. We must become students of our children's personalities to discover how best to build them up. In my family, for example, Alexandra responds more to affection and encouragement, whereas Elizabeth is inspired by challenging goals.

Showing favoritism and comparing

Let's say you have two sons—one is an athlete, the other a musician. Do you applaud the achievements of one more than the other? Some of us do, simply because of our personal preference. Or you have two daughters—one is a straight-A genius, and the other is an average student but is a leader, and is very active in service clubs. If you try to challenge either one by comparison to the other, you will breed frustration, jealousy and bitterness. Instead, appreciate and commend the strengths of both.

Pushing too hard, too soon

If you are a highly motivated achiever, be careful that you do not burn your kids out before they hit the third grade! They *are*

133

children, you know! In my four years coaching soccer, I saw some parents ranting and raving on the sidelines, pushing their kids as if their 10-year-olds were playing for the World Cup. I always told them: "Look, they are kids. They are here to learn soccer, to make friends, to learn how to be team players, and to have fun. Believe me, we are going to try our best to win. But please, *let them be kids!*" I was one of the most fired-up coaches in the league, but it was the fire of zeal, not anger. My teams won two championships and were in the playoffs the other two years, and we had fun doing it! Some of you have children that could be outstanding in dance, sports, grades, etc., but you have literally driven them away from these things by pressuring them too much.

One more observation: If you have kids who are very immature emotionally and/or physically and who are near the calendar cut-off, it may be better to hold them back a year before first grade. We did this with our two boys and have never regretted it.

Parental self-degradation

If you verbally downgrade yourself in front of your children, you hurt their view of life and of themselves. They will imitate you in viewing their faults as being greater than their strengths. At our house, this kind of talk is strictly off-limits for everyone.

Living our lives through our children

Let God guide your offspring into the path he chooses for them. Don't try to make up for all you failed to accomplish by pushing your kids into things they don't really care about. I wish I had played more organized sports as a youngster, but I refuse to pressure my boys into it on my account. I have tried to encourage and inspire them in athletics but they have no feeling that "Dad will be disappointed if I don't do awesome in sports." Give guidance and direction, but please, keep your pride out of the picture!

The Right Foundation

The only proper foundation for a child's confidence is his or her relationship to God. If they look to God and his unconditional love, they will develop a confidence that is not cocky and a humility that is not self-hatred.

> And so we know and rely on the love God has for us...Love is made complete among us so that we will have confidence on the day of judgment...There is no fear in love. But perfect love drives out fear... (1 John 4:16-18).

How to Nurture Confidence

Here is a list of nine practical helps to building godly self-esteem:

Stress relationship to God

Teach them that they are special in God's sight and that he is with them in all they do.

Focus on character above looks, talent, intelligence and possessions

Over and over again, tell your children that it is heart and attitude that matter most to God. I have a saying: "Character always wins out in the end." Talented kids may dazzle their way to the top, but without character, they will come crashing back down.

Applaud effort more than ability or achievement

In the parable of the talents (Matthew 25) three men were given different amounts of money, each according to his differing ability. The two successful men were equally commended by the master even though one produced more than the other. Let it be so in your home!

Encourage openness about their fears, insecurities and failures

Kids are often burdened with anxieties or a sense of total failure. They may hide it from you and even from themselves. Watch, listen, notice. *Ask* them if they have anything on their minds that they need to talk about. When they open up to you, work them through things until they are confident. I have found that sharing some of my more famous blunders and failures as a youngster helps my kids to see that *everyone* makes mistakes. Their faces light up, and they say "Dad, did that really happen? What did you do about it?" This draws me closer to my kids and assures them that they are not alone.

Encourage achievement and provide opportunities to grow in their areas of natural strength

Search out your kids' strengths, and develop them! *Everyone* has been gifted by God in some area, yet so many people go through life thinking they have no talent. Others make Herculean efforts to succeed, but in a field that is removed from their sphere of ability. No matter how hard they try, they come up average simply because they are out-of-pocket. Your job is to help your children discover and succeed in those things for which they are best suited.

Help them improve in areas of weakness

Encourage your children to be well-rounded. Don't let them totally withdraw because they feel inadequate or awkward. For example, your children may not be the best students—their talent may lie in athletics or in people skills. Don't let them give up on their grades and just become a "jock" or a popularity freak. Academics are too important to neglect simply because they don't come easily. The same thing is true of other areas as well.

When I think of the great men and women of the Bible, I see people who had excellent talents but broadened themselves so that they could make a better contribution. Consider the woman of Proverbs 31, whose skills ranged from homemaking to business and management; consider David who was a shepherd, soldier, military commander, political leader, songwriter, musician and singer. Encourage your children to have their special expertise but to be interested and knowledgeable in many things.

Help them form upbuilding friendships

The circle of friends around your child can build or break confidence. All young people need to belong to a group that affirms and accepts them. It is devastating for a child never to fit in or to always feel inferior and on the "outs." Some kids try to hook up with groups or individuals that basically do not accept them and constantly put them down. If you see this happening, you need either to teach your children how to act differently, so as to not turn people off, or you need to steer them towards a different group.

Don't be afraid to monitor your children's friendships. We have always told our kids, "If you can't help someone be better, or if either one of you makes the other a worse person, then you cannot be friends." We have said it, and we have enforced it. We have an obligation, especially with younger ones, to protect our children from the tease, the bully, the kid who ridicules or the child who is a bad influence.

David once had a friend like this in our neighborhood. The kid was not intimidating or threatening, he was just critical of David all the time. He was a year older, and therefore was stronger, faster and more coordinated. He would point this out and take digs at David for not being able to match his awesome feats. It was done quietly and subtly, but I finally noticed what was going on. I talked to this boy about it—with David there. I pointed out that his own older brother was better than he at things, but that this was to be expected because of their age difference. Later, I pulled David aside and confronted the issue directly, asking him if he felt bad about himself. He assured me that all the talk didn't bother him, but I still urged him never to let it hurt his confidence. Geri and I started monitoring the relationship more, and we diminished the amount of time the two boys spent together. We encouraged David to play with kids his own age and provided more opportunities for that to occur.

Through the years, all of our children have had friendships with wholesome kids from excellent families in the church. We have made the effort to overcome any obstacles of distance or inconvenience to make this happen, and it has paid off. Even when someone moves, we encourage the keeping up of these friendships by phone, letters and special visits. These relationships with other "Kingdom Kids" are incredible in their influence for good in our children's spirituality, happiness and confidence.

Teach them to appreciate and applaud the efforts and achievements of others

Children who learn to admire and encourage others will be confident. They are strong enough to give credit when credit is due. They see that others are not always their rivals but are their friends and companions. Competition is good, but always having to win is bad. Nobody likes a sore loser who whines, sulks and gets angry when defeated; nor do people like a cocky winner who rubs it in when victorious.

Teach your kids to give their best and never to blame the teacher, their teammates, referees and/or selection committees when they lose. If they can "rejoice with those who rejoice," they will learn to accept themselves, accept life, and still be confident.

Teach your kids the example of young men like Jonathan, who could have easily been jealous of David, but who instead became his best friend and greatest encourager (1 Samuel 18). Teach them about John the Baptist who said that Jesus had to become greater, and he had to become lesser (John 3:30).

Be basically encouraging

Be your children's biggest fan! Expect great things! Tell them they are awesome—and they will be! Praise the little pictures they bring home; look at, and encourage them in their homework; go to their games and recitals; attend their awards assemblies; let them feel the tremendous warmth and backing that only a parent can give. If you are fundamentally positive, then even when you do give correction, it will be received with thankfulness rather than discouragement. Someone has said that it takes five compliments to overcome one criticism. I don't know the exact numbers, but I do know that human nature flourishes with a diet of praise and that it shrivels when fed with continual blame. If your kids feel they have your blessing and approval, their confidence will soar!

❧

In Psalm 23 David speaks of the faith he had as a boy. "The Lord is my shepherd, I shall not be in want" (Psalm 23:1). What confidence, what assurance, what peace resided in this young man's heart!

It is no wonder, then, that when the great moment of challenge came, as Goliath stood defiantly before the cowed army of God, that this courageous, innocent teenage hero rose up. He based his confidence upon the victories of his boyhood: "The Lord who delivered me from the paw of the lion and the paw of the bear will deliver me from the hand of this Philistine" (1 Samuel 17:37). The connection is obvious. The faith he developed in the simplicity of his youth was the quality which catapulted him to greater things. *He prepared himself, and his moment came.*

Build that kind of confidence into your sons and daughters, stand back and watch what God will do!

FABRIC

CHAPTER 9

Foundations of a Spiritual Family

But as for you, continue in what you have learned and have become convinced of, because you know those from whom you learned it, and how from infancy you have known the holy Scriptures, which are able to make you wise for salvation through faith in Christ Jesus (2 Timothy 3:14-15).

What do we mean when we talk about "a spiritual family"? Perhaps we should begin by discussing what we mean by the term "spiritual," and go from there.

Paul uses this word to describe a level of maturity that is beyond the early, immature stages of discipleship when we still think, react and behave more as we did before we became disciples of Jesus (1 Corinthians 3:1-4). He also says that those "who are spiritual" are capable of restoring Christians who have fallen into sin and are able to "carry each other's burdens..." (Galatians 6:1-2). Although Jesus does not use the term "spiritual" in the Sermon on the Mount, the teaching he gave there is a perfect definition of what it means to have this great quality. Simply put, it means to *be* on the inside what we are trying to *do* on the outside: to be genuine, not to live a pretense of religious performance but to function out of a sincere relationship with God.

A spiritual family, then, is a family where God is honored and where his presence is sought and experienced in daily life. It is a home where prayer is an ongoing reality and where the Bible is faithfully read and obeyed. It is a family who honors God with a total commitment of life and heart—a family that is dedicated to following Christ. It is a home that loves God's church and is fully involved in its fellowship and ministry. It is a family who has times of worship, praise and study. It is a place where the children have their own times of personal Bible study and where the parents spend regular times with each child to disciple them to Christ. And finally, it is a group that is dedicated to helping others become disciples of Jesus.

This is much more than a "good" family, a "nice" family or even a church-going family. A family can be all of those things and still not be spiritual. To be spiritual is far more real and infinitely more powerful. A spiritual family is the "salt of the earth," "the light of the world," "a city set on a hill," whose example is so inspiring that other people notice and give glory to God. To be a spiritual family is a wonderful and powerful thing.

A spiritual family must be led by spiritual parents. We cannot take our families where we ourselves have not gone. As was pointed out in Chapter 1, children can spot a fake a mile away. Therefore, we must be genuine in our love for God, consistent in our walk with him, and wholehearted in our dedication to his cause if we are to have any impact upon our kids.

What are the things we must incorporate into family life if we are to be spiritual? We will discuss six basic areas: prayer, discipling times, family devotionals, devotion to the church, an evangelistic lifestyle and children's quiet times.

1. Prayer

As parents, we should pray *for* our children continually. We should lift up our children before the throne of God always, praying that he might protect them, guide them, save them, and one day take them to heaven. We should imitate Paul, who said of his prayers for Timothy, his son in the faith, "...night and day I constantly remember you in my prayers" (2 Timothy 1:3). We must realize that we have a powerful and relentless adversary who wants to destroy us and our family as well! He will stop at *nothing* to take our children away from God. Our prayers are perhaps the most powerful weapon available in their spiritual defense.

I am reminded of Jesus' words to Peter on the night of his betrayal and arrest, when knowing that Peter would confront the full power of Satan, he warned him:

> "Simon, Simon, Satan has asked to sift you as wheat. But I have prayed for you, Simon, that your faith may not fail. And when you have turned back, strengthen your brothers" (Luke 22:31-32).

"But I have prayed for you." These words of Jesus show the difference prayer can make in the battle for the souls of our loved ones. Parents, we need to be prayer warriors on behalf of our children! We are in a battle for their souls, and our prayers can turn the tide!

But we must pray *with* our children as well. They will learn to pray by hearing us pray. They will learn to feel God's presence as they see it is real to us. We should pray with our children at regular times such as bedtime and mealtime—not in a rote or routine manner but from the heart. Geri and I often pray with our kids as they step out the front door on the way to school. In our home in Miami, this developed into a neighborhood event. The other young boys on our street began to notice what we were doing and gathered around our front door every morning to join in our family prayers as they headed off to school. (Don't tell me that kids don't want to pray!) We also have family prayer just before we get out of the car to go into church services. It helps everyone get into the right frame of mind. Since Geri and I often have speaking assignments, we ask the kids to pray for us. I'll never forget one of the prayers of my son Jonathan: "Dear God, help my dad to do an awesome sermon, and please God, help him to *think* he did an awesome sermon!" (You see, my son knows all too well that I am my own worst critic!)

In times of difficulty or great challenge, the family should be in prayer together. The children learn that we are totally dependent on God to help us and that we can do nothing without his blessing. One way we accomplish this in our family is by setting up "prayer partners." I recently had it on my heart to meet someone myself whom I could help lead to Christ before the year was out. I knew I would need God's power in a special way, so I got my youngest, Alexandra, to be my prayer partner for this particular request. I asked her what I could pray about for her. She gazed at me with that special five-year-old "little girl look" and said, "Daddy, please pray that I will respect my brother Jonathan more." I started praying for her and she for me. In just a few short months, a couple that Geri and I met in our apartment complex became disciples! Needless to say, Alexandra was thrilled! Her faith is much greater now and so is mine. (And yes, Alexandra has improved in showing respect for her brother!)

What if you have a young child who does not want to pray at bedtime? We have faced this from time to time with our kids, and my wife has developed some strategies that always seem to work. First, she talks about how God is a real "person" who loves them and wants to be close to them, and that even though they cannot see God, he is always nearby. If the resistance to praying keeps up, Geri says, "Well, if you don't want to pray, then you're probably too tired for your bedtime song as well. Good night. I'll see you in the morning!" That always does it! It's amazing how quickly the kids get motivated to pray when Mom handles it this way.

2. Discipling Times

Simply put, discipling times are the set times you spend alone with your children to talk with them, teach them the Bible, and pray with them. You may begin to have them as soon as your child is able to communicate fairly well, although it will obviously be on a very limited scale—just a short Bible verse and prayer is all he or she needs. As children get older, you can gradually lengthen the time, although it should never go too long for their limited attention span. *Never* let discipling times become a boring, burdensome duty! They should always be fun, exciting times of learning and closeness for both of you.

I try to go someplace out of the house, even if just for a walk in the neighborhood. Sometimes I take the kids to the park, or we go to a fast-food restaurant and get a soft drink. Because of the special challenges of her schedule, Geri usually has her times at home. We try to have them at set hours, although with a large, busy family we have to be flexible. Since we have four kids, we try to split things up to make sure each of them has a discipling time with one of us each week.

We select topics and verses to help the children with their current needs. Geri and I will often compare notes to help each other determine what the needs are. The kids and I then read the verses together, talk about them, and decide what action to take. Many times we will commit some part of the Scripture to memory. At dinner anyone who has had a "D-time" that day usually will share it with the whole family.

I try to let God lead these talks in the direction he wants. Many times I select a topic but then realize that the kids need to talk about something else. Whatever we talk about, I *always* bring the subject back around to the Scriptures and make an application. We then close out with a prayer together.

The value of these times is absolutely incalculable. They have drawn my children closer to God and to me. I urge you, if you have not done so already, to establish these great times as a consistent part of your family life immediately!

3. Family Devotionals

> From there he went on toward the hills east of Bethel and pitched his tent, with Bethel on the west and Ai on the east. There he built an altar to the Lord and called on the name of the Lord. Then Abram set out and continued toward the Negev (Genesis 12:8-9).

Family worship is an absolute must if we are to build a spiritual household. These are those wonderful times when the entire family gathers to sing, pray, study the Bible, draw near to one another and worship God. It is a chance to have our own worship service—to be a small church. There is no feeling quite like gathering in our own home with those we love most in all the world to draw near to God together. When we do, we know that the Lord himself is with us, as he promised:

> "Again, I tell you that if two of you on earth agree about anything you ask for, it will be done for you by my Father in heaven. For where two or three come together in my name, there am I with them" (Matthew 18:19-20).

What a wonderful promise, and what a beautiful experience for a family to have! We have had guests in for our devotionals from time to time, and they always have gone away deeply moved by the sense of spiritual power and reality that they felt from being with us. It is God's desire for all families to experience the greatness of worshiping him together. It can literally turn the entire atmosphere of a home for the better.

Family devotionals should be anything but a boring, irrelevant hour to be endured by dutiful parents and restless children. Not at all! They should be dynamic, joyful, fun, down-to-earth and creative. Now that's a tall order for some of us parents! This means that we need to plan the devotional with our spouses, being careful to select a subject relevant to the current needs of the family. Never, never just go through the motions! Use the time to address any important behavior or attitude issue. This is not to say that we should always use the time correcting everyone. If you allow your family devotional to turn into a weekly tongue-lashing of the kids, you will have taken out the positive, joyful energy. It can be a time to confront, but let it be primarily an opportunity to teach, train and inspire. Use it to paint a picture of the way things should be and *will* be by the power of God.

Our family devotionals last about 45 minutes. Geri and I usually plan them, but sometimes we sit back and allow the kids to plan and lead the whole devotional themselves. We have a pattern we generally follow, but we never allow ourselves to get into a rut. We usually begin with 10-20 minutes of singing. My sons and I handle this part, and as they have grown older, they have taken more and more of the lead. We vary the selections from the high-energy praise songs to the most beautiful hymns of worship. Sometimes we even break out the songbooks and teach the kids the old toe-tapper "gospel" songs or the devotional songs from our early campus ministry days. Next comes the lesson. I usually lead it and seek to draw out plenty of discussion. On many occasions we will do role-playing and act out Bible stories. We close out with prayer, usually with everyone having a chance to join in.

Our topics for devotionals have covered every conceivable subject. We have studied many of the parables and incidents in Jesus' life. On one occasion we discussed Jesus' teaching on being servant-leader in Matthew 20:20-28 and declared the following week to be "servant's week." We have acted out many of the great Old Testament stories, such as Aaron and Hur holding up Moses' arms to win victory in battle (Exodus 17:8-13). We used it to teach the need for unity and encouragement. We have acted out the four kinds of disobedience (defiant, disarming, deaf and dreary) that we shared with you in Chapter 6 of this book.

One night we centered the whole devotional on the topic of "respect." Frankly, I was aiming it mostly at our youngest, Alexandra, who at age four seemed to be having a hard time giving her brother Jonathan the respect due him as her older sibling. We went through elaborate acting parts and taught the scriptures about respecting each other. I felt as if I had done a masterful job and that now Alexandra would just be a perfect model of the submissive younger sister. I approached her the next day and asked, "Honey, what did you learn at family devotional last night?" fully expecting to hear of her new-found repentance. Without the slightest hesitation she looked up, smiled, and said proudly, "I learned that everybody in this whole family needs to respect *me*!" Needless to say, we had to back up and try again the next week!

4. Devotion to the Church

The Bible teaches to "love the brotherhood of believers" (1 Peter 2:17). The church is God's family and is the place in which we serve him on a day-to-day basis. It follows then, that we should love God's church ourselves and that we should cultivate that same love in our families.

If you have positive, loving attitudes about the church, your kids will, too. In my family, the kids know that we love God's people and that we love to be at church activities. I cannot think of one time that our kids have developed bad attitudes about attending church services. On the contrary, they love to go! Their best friends are there. They love the worship services, and they enjoy their Bible classes. If we have ever noticed that things were not being done excellently in the kid's ministry, we have pitched in and helped to make it better. I would urge you to do the same. Don't sit back and say, "Why doesn't somebody do this better?" Make it better yourself!

Teach your kids to respect their Bible class teachers and to honor and appreciate their youth or teen workers. These people should be their heroes! If they have a conflict with a leader or with another kid at church, make sure they solve it quickly. Don't let them become outsiders, malcontents or troublemakers in the youth group.

If you ever have a problem with someone or something at church, solve it in a godly way—don't speak inappropriately in front of your kids about it. If you do, you will undermine your children's love for God's kingdom, and you will reap a bitter harvest from what you have sown!

5. An Evangelistic Lifestyle

Sharing the good news of Jesus should be a natural part of our everyday lives, something our whole family thinks about constantly. The kids should feel tremendously blessed to be in a Christian home and should be eager to help other families to learn about God.

In our household, the kids all want our family to impact other families for Christ. We all prayed for several months recently that our family could be instrumental in bringing another family to the Lord. Our prayers were answered! Our son Jonathan invited a young friend from our apartment complex to church. He came, and eventually his whole family started attending as well. The husband and wife studied the Bible with me, Geri, and some other people from our church, and in a few weeks' time, they became Christians! Their oldest son is now studying to become a disciple. Each of our children had a role in reaching this family. They came to love Alexandra, our youngest, who went downstairs several evenings a week to help prepare their dinner (she was actually getting free cooking lessons!); our boys spent time playing sports with their sons; and Elizabeth was always there, setting a great example of what a Christian teenager should be. We all were used by God in some way to make the difference! And when our friends were baptized into Christ, the Laing kids were there, each having felt a part of something really great!

Too many of us have separated our families from our outreach to others. We have forgotten that our families are the brightest light that God can use to illuminate a dark world. It literally blows people away when they see a happy, loving family with respectful, obedient kids. It is so rare!

Have people into your home. Let them meet your children. Draw people into your family life. They will see what is there and will want to have it for themselves. When they do, teach them where it comes from! And when they do accept it, they will stick it out because they are so strongly tied in with great family relationships in God's church.

6. Children's Quiet Times

Early in life, children need to cultivate their own relationships with God. He must become real to them, a friend and companion who loves them, is always with them, and who constantly watches over them. For children raised in Christian homes, the great danger is that they will go through the motions of going to church services and attending all the functions available to them but not have a personal heart for God. Having their own quiet times is one of the best ways for them to learn to know God and enjoy him personally.

The quiet time spent alone with the Bible and in prayer provides children the opportunity to develop their own faith. Kids in deeply committed churches hear so much challenge to commitment that it can become overwhelming to them. They must come to know and love the one who is issuing the call to commitment! Geri and I have taught our kids to use the quiet moments alone with God to come to know him for who he is. We have urged them to go outside, to look around at the beauties of nature, and realize that God made it all—that he is powerful, wise, and yet very concerned for them as individuals. This has helped our kids to look at God as someone who can be loved as a friend and not just as a master who wants their obedience.

In the younger years of preschool and early elementary school, you should sit down a couple of mornings a week and have brief quiet times with your children, teaching them how to go about it. As they get older, in later elementary school age, they can begin to have them on their own. We recommend that kids start out spending about 10 minutes per session, divided between prayer and Bible study. Teach them to keep a private journal where they write down the things they learn. At first, give plenty of guidance including the specific scriptures they need to study each day and a prayer list. It helps if you teach kids to pray with some sort of pattern. We have found the A.C.T.S. pattern to work well for kids: Adoration, Confession, Thanksgiving and Supplication. Be sure to go through each topic, explain exactly what it means, and how to pray in that area.

As your children get older, direct them to study books like Proverbs, Psalms and the Gospels. Have them study the lives of the youth and teens of the Bible such as Joseph, Samuel, David, Daniel, Miriam and Mary. Always keep up with how it is going to make sure they are continuing to learn and aren't getting bored. If that happens, give them some ideas to help them make things exciting again. (The children's quiet-time books published as part of the Kingdom Kids Series by Discipleship Publications International make excellent resources. The kids love having their own books and get excited about answering the questions.)

There are many variables in all of this that cannot be addressed in this book. You will have to study the personalities and characters of your children to determine their levels of maturity and spiritual readiness. You can make a mistake either way: By pushing them ahead too quickly, you can overwhelm your kids; by not challenging them enough, you leave a vacuum in their hearts that can be filled up by the world. Pray for wisdom, get wise counsel from spiritual people, and trust God to guide you!

153

❦

These are the building blocks to use in constructing a spiritual household. It is our prayer that God will use these teachings to help you lead your family to spiritual strength and to a genuine walk with God.

CHAPTER 10

A Close Family

...his brothers...hated him and could not speak a kind word to him (Genesis 37:4).

How good and pleasant it is when brothers live together in unity! (Psalm 133:1).

I ONCE ASKED A POLICEMAN FRIEND OF MINE WHAT SITUATION faced in the line of duty frightened him the most. I expected to hear something about drug busts or armed robbery, but instead, the reply I received was "domestic conflict." Yes, domestic conflict! At first I was surprised, but after thinking about it for a while, I realized the truth of his words.

Is there any place on earth where our passions run deeper and our weaknesses are exposed more than in our own homes? It is here, with those closest to us, that our nerves become raw and our hearts become embittered. It is in the home, where we have given our deepest love, that the hurts penetrate the most painfully.

I would encourage you to sit back sometime and listen to what is being said under your own roof. Turn on a tape recorder,

155

place it in a corner, and forget it is on. Play it back later and note carefully what you hear. Listen to the words and to the tones of voice. I am sure that most of us would be amazed and ashamed to know how we, and our children, address one another.

Let's face it—*most families are not that close.* Tension, bickering and quarreling rule. There are explosive arguments and simmering feuds that go unresolved indefinitely. And even if there is not much outward conflict, many families merely exist together without any deep love or enjoyment of one another. If fighting and bitterness is the downfall of some families, shallowness and superficiality is the cancer that slowly consumes the souls of others.

Even when we search the Scriptures for answers, we find more of the same. Consider the story of Cain and Abel, the first murder in history, committed by a man's own brother! Look at Jacob and his twin brother Esau, set at odds by the folly of their parents' favoritism and driven from one another by their greed, envy and desire for revenge. See how the sin continues into the next generation as Jacob's sons turn against their younger brother Joseph, conspire to send him away as a slave and cover over their plot with the fabrication of his accidental death, leaving their father heartbroken in grief for years. Look at the family of David, torn apart by lust, rape and incest, with one brother murdering another and then leading a rebellion to take away his father's throne. Do we need to see any more to convince us of the horror of a divided house? It is as if God is saying, "I will give you an answer to your problem, but I first want you to see how terrible and awful are the consequences of a disunited and warring family." It ought to cause us to humble ourselves, get the help we need, and make the changes we must make.

Thank God, there is a way out! Things can be different if parents decide to make them different. For some of us, it will mean a radical change in what we accept and in what we expect. But with prayer, proper discipling of the kids and determination, it will happen!

There are four keys to having a close family, and we will discuss each one in turn. The keys are respect, openness, fabric and atmosphere.

1. Respect

We discussed the importance of children's respect for parents in Chapter 5, but here we refer to respect that must exist among everyone in the entire household. How can we have it?

Eliminate critical, harsh talk

I am shocked by the kind of talk that is allowed in some of our homes. For some of us, it has gone on so long that we are desensitized to its brutality. We have never repented of the manner of speaking that we engaged in back in the world. Our conversations sound more like the "slash and burn" of a TV sitcom than that of a godly Christian household. It is as if we accept this as normal—we admit that the Bible says otherwise, but we think that its teachings are an unattainable ideal. So we do not even make the effort to change. To this I say, God forbid that any disciple of Jesus Christ would *ever* dismiss or ignore the Scriptures! Let us listen to these verses and take them to heart:

> Reckless words pierce like a sword, but the tongue of the wise brings healing (Proverbs 12:18).

> A man who lacks judgment derides his neighbor, but a man of understanding holds his tongue (Proverbs 11:12).

> A gentle answer turns away wrath, but a harsh word stirs up anger (Proverbs 15:1).

> Do not let any unwholesome talk come out of your mouths, but only what is helpful for building others up according to their needs, that it may benefit those who listen. Do not

> grieve the Holy Spirit of God, with whom you were sealed
> for the day of redemption. Get rid of all bitterness, rage
> and anger, brawling and slander, along with every form of
> malice. Be kind and compassionate to one another,
> forgiving each other, just as in Christ God forgave you
> (Ephesians 4:29-32).

Paul says there are some things we just plain need to "get rid of." No fanfare, no playing around, no psychobabble—just *get rid of them*.

We must get rid of harsh *words*. Words like "stupid," "dumb" and "shut up" must go! Some of you are using and permitting far worse language than this, language that I cannot put in print. There is no excuse for this. God will judge you for using it and for allowing it under your roof.

> "But I tell you that men will have to give account on the day
> of judgment for every careless word they have spoken. For
> by your words you will be acquitted, and by your words
> you will be condemned" (Matthew 12:36-37).

To all of us I say, it is time to get serious about changing our language. Name-calling is absolutely wrong and must be removed completely from the realm of possibility in our homes. We think it's all right because no one hears it except our family members. What a pathetic double standard! Let me ask you, would you use the same words if Jesus were in the room? Let that be the test!

We must get rid of harsh *tones of voice*. We need to remember the words of Paul, who told us that love "is not rude" (1 Corinthians 13:5). A sneering tone, dripping with scorn, contempt and sarcasm is just as wrong as cursing someone. Many of us speak this way as a matter of habit, and we allow it to go on among the kids as well. Some kids can make a supposedly harmless statement like, "Please pass the salt," at the dinner table with enough venom to kill. This must be stopped, and it *can* be stopped!

We must get rid of harsh *actions, looks and expressions.* Communication is far, far more than words and voice—it is done with the entire body. Slamming doors, throwing things, stomping feet—all say much more than words what we really feel. The Bible talks about "haughty eyes," and it says that God detests them (Proverbs 6:16-17). When the kids roll their eyes at us or at one another, it is a sign of contempt and disrespect. It must be recognized, confronted and eliminated from their behavior.

Cultivate genuine appreciation

This is the second major step in building respect into your family life. In the previous section we addressed what we must be rid of; now we speak of how to put the good in place of the evil that we have removed.

This is something to tackle in our family devotional times. Geri and I, in our family nights, have taught our children countless lessons on mutual respect. We have studied just about every story and verse we can find to illustrate this all-important habit of thought and behavior. It will not come about in your family by accident! You must teach it, talk about how to show it, and confront the ways the kids are not expressing it. This is the only way! We have worked long and hard on this, and it has paid off in dividends of peace and joy in our home that are beyond price.

The most consistent positive comment we get about our kids is that they are respectful—not only to adults, but to one another. Just the other day as we were finishing lunch at a restaurant, a woman at a table adjacent to our three youngest children (the three of them were sitting together at their own table) stopped me as we made our way up to the cash register. She said, "I don't know what you are doing in raising your kids, but I have never seen such well-behaved children. Your sons, without anyone telling them to, even shared their pie with their younger sister!" She also mentioned that she had found it necessary to be moved to another location in the restaurant earlier because of a table of unruly children arguing next to her.

We get comments like this fairly often from people within and without the church. This tells me that the behavior Geri and I consider normal is not considered to be so in other families! The fact is, our kids are no better or worse than anyone else's. It is simply a matter of what we have trained and expected. And in case you are wondering, our kids are not stuffy little do-gooders who don't ever make mistakes or cut loose and have a good time. We are talking about an *attitude* of respect for each other that, due to biblical teaching, has become second nature.

Another way to cultivate respect in the home is to create as many situations as possible where it is expressed in words. Again, this is where family devotionals are invaluable. We often have entire sessions focused upon "building up one another." We go around the circle, and each person encourages every other person specifically. We urge the kids to be creative in their observations and to cite ways they have seen one another (and Mom and Dad!) change and grow. We have "thank you nights" when all we do is give thanks for different things other family members have said and done. Usually there are spontaneous hugs and tears of joy that flow in these times. I have often found myself as encouraged and inspired after one of these devotionals as after attending a powerful worship service of the whole church.

God made us to flourish under respect, appreciation and encouragement. Encourage your family to begin expressing these things, and watch the whole atmosphere change to one of joy and brightness!

> Pleasant words are a honeycomb, sweet to the soul and
> healing to the bones (Proverbs 16:24).

One last brief piece of advice before we leave the topic of respect: Teach your older children how to lead, and teach your younger ones how to follow. We have spent much time and effort training our two oldest, Elizabeth and David, how to be good leaders of the younger children. It has proved extremely helpful in that the older ones have been able to take care of their younger siblings effectively, thus creating a more relaxed and peaceful home: more relaxed because Geri and I are able to trust that things will go well when we are not around, and more peaceful because the younger ones happily accept the leadership of their older brother and sister. A major part of the training has been done in working with the younger ones. We have had to teach them to respect the delegated authority of their older siblings, even though Elizabeth's and David's leadership skills are obviously not as effective as ours.

We have discovered that our children's weaknesses tend to come out more with each other than with us. This includes the weaknesses of the older and younger ones. We have been able to do much more effective discipling when we have put our kids in this situation, and it has contributed immensely to their own growth and respect for each other. Now we are busy training Jonathan and Alexandra how to have the same leader-follower dynamic in their relationship as well.

2. Openness

> Instead, speaking the truth in love, we will in all things grow up into him who is the Head, that is, Christ (Ephesians 4:15).

An open family is a close family. If there is no simmering backlog of unresolved problems, issues and conflicts, a family can be united. Our children should feel absolutely confident to bring up to us anything on their minds, at any time they feel the need. Many of us do not realize the frustration and desperation that exists in our children's hearts because they do not feel free to talk with us.

Our children must believe, first of all, that we care enough about them to give them our full attention. Second, they must know that if it is something unpleasant, we will not fly off the handle in anger before they have a chance to tell the whole story. If they know these two things, then we have established an open-door policy with them that is absolutely invaluable.

What do kids need to talk about? Younger children have a myriad of things going through their little heads that you need to help them with. They may have hurt feelings, and you may be the one that did the hurting! They may have an ongoing difficulty with one of their siblings or with a playmate that you can help them solve. They could have a problem with their school work or with a teacher, or a bully may be picking on them. They might have something on their consciences from days past that they never have been able to confess. Their needs will range from the trivial to the gravely serious—and you need to hear them all!

What about older children? I have news for you—as children grow up, it only gets more intense! That is why the paragraph above is so important—the sooner you start, the better. The issues older kids deal with include dating, sex, drugs, temptations, weird thoughts, grades, appearance and issues involving their conversion. It is a wonderful thing to sit down and talk with your children about all of the things on their minds, and it will draw you much closer to them.

But the need for openness is not limited to parents with the children—it also includes the children with one another. In working with adults, I am amazed at how many are emotionally separated from their brothers and sisters, and how far back in their lives those conflicts go. Geri and I have always made it our practice never to allow conflicts between our kids to go unsettled. As soon as we become aware of a problem, we send the kids off together to talk it out. It has always worked. Sometimes we have had to mediate, but usually the kids, completely on their own, have emerged from these talks smiling, happy and completely reconciled.

If we allow a child to brood, carry resentments, and hold in his or her feelings, we will find ourselves sitting on a time bomb. It will go off sooner or later, and everyone in the family will be hurt!

Consider for a moment the stories of two of the most tragic figures of the Bible, King Saul and Judas Iscariot. Saul was a brooding, tormented man who was filled with jealousy and envy. Instead of working through his temptations honestly, he held in his feelings. A reading of 1 Samuel 18 reveals that his pattern was to think one thing, but to say another. (Does that describe any of your children?) His turmoil increased, resulting in his complete emotional and spiritual breakdown.

With Judas, we have a similar story. Read through the Gospels, and look for the words of Judas. There are virtually none. Contrast that with Peter, who was completely outspoken and whose words got him in trouble on just about every page! Both men had their weaknesses, but which one overcame them? The one who was open! As parents we should be more concerned about the child who holds everything in than the one who lets it all out. The latter can be helped, but the former is isolated and lonely as his or her problems go unsolved.

Have open talks during your family devotional times. Keep the air clear. Keep it clear with every individual and with the whole group as well. Establish an atmosphere of freedom and openness. You will not lose authority by hearing what is on everyone's minds; you will instead create a happy, relaxed and righteous family.

3. Fabric

By fabric I refer to building a structure and a rhythm into our family schedules. For families to be close, they must have regular times when the whole group gets together. During those hours we build an identity and a feeling of our own little society that is just "us." It is this feeling of group togetherness that makes a family a family, and that makes being in it one of the most joyous experiences on earth.

I am afraid that many of us do not even know what this is like. We never experienced it in our homes growing up, and we do not really know exactly what we're shooting for now. But don't be discouraged! If we try, we can learn!

When and how can we create a fabric for our families that will hold them tightly together? Let me suggest several ways to go about it.

Use mealtimes

We all have to eat somewhere, sometime. Why not do it together? It is a natural time to stop what we are doing, gather around the table, sit down, enjoy a nice meal, and have a great time being with one another.

My family loves mealtimes. We always eat dinner together. Because of the different schedules of the kids' schools, having breakfast and lunch together is not possible. That leaves dinner. Geri usually cooks the meal, and sometimes I do if we are having barbecue. If we order out, it is because we are having a special movie and pizza night or because our schedules have been unusually busy.

Everyone is there for dinner. If someone is missing, there is a very good reason. We all sit down to eat at the same time. We begin with a prayer. We talk with each other during the meal. The television is off. The phone answering machine is on, with the volume turned down so we are not interrupted. We have an awesome time! All of us have plenty to talk about—we even save up things to share with the family during dinnertime.

Sometimes, the conversation gets a little disjointed, and we are not as "together" as we should be. On one such occasion a few years ago, when Jonathan was around two, he was feeling left out, and to get back in the middle of things, he turned to me and asked, "So, Daddy, what did *you* do today?" We all got the point, and it has led to what is our standard practice now. Usually at any given meal, we all get around to telling the significant things that happened to us during the day. I can't begin to tell you how close this has made our family.

This seems so simple, doesn't it? It seems that way, and it is! But the simple things are what build fabric into a family, and they are the stuff of which memories are made.

Please, stop feeding everybody out of paper bags or just leaving the food on the stove for people to serve themselves whenever they have a chance. Stop letting people read the paper, watch TV, or do their homework during dinner. Disallow the grabbing of plates and running off to eat in separate rooms. Stop setting up appointments that take you away from your family during the evening meal. Allow no more phone calls during this hour! Make dinnertime an event, work hard to keep it special, and watch your family draw closer!

Create family traditions

There ought to be some things that our families do that are uniquely "ours" and that bond us together in a special way. These things don't have to be expensive or elaborate, nor do they have to take up large amounts of time. But they do have to be activities that everyone loves to do, and that we all do together. Families who have these kinds of things going on are close.

My family loves it when I make pancakes on Saturday mornings. I can't always do this because there is usually quite a bit of activity scheduled on Saturdays. But whenever I can, and everyone is there, it's a blast! As each of the children has come along, they have helped me prepare the batter. I will always treasure the memories of each one sitting on the kitchen counter, helping me hold the electric beaters, and singing songs with me as we worked together. I really don't put anything special into the recipe, but I always get rave reviews. Geri especially loves

"Pancake Time," because she doesn't have to do a thing, except enjoy the food and fellowship!

This is just one example of the many traditions our family has developed over the years. We never sat down and decided what they were going to be, or when—they just kind of invented themselves! I would urge you to begin some family traditions. And if you have been neglecting the ones you already have, start a revival!

Holidays and birthdays

We should look through our Bibles and check out all of the special feast days and celebrations that God planned every year for his people. Do we get the point? We need holidays, those special times of being together that our families can look forward to all year long.

My family loves Christmas. Now I know that some people have qualms about not knowing the precise date of Jesus' birth, and I know that others just choose not to make Christmas a big deal, but our family does—and do we ever! The kids have a scripted set of moves that we must follow, just in going out to buy the tree! After we bring it home, we have a chili dinner. Next, I put on the lights, then Mom and the kids put on the rest of the decorations. After the tree is all done, we turn out the lights in the rest of the house, plug in the lights on the tree, sit in front of our beautiful handiwork, and have an eggnog toast. Folks, this is just a sampling of the many family traditions we have during Christmas! I won't burden you with all the others, but, be assured, Christmas is one of the most special memories our family carries with us, year in and year out, and the memories of those special times will be with us forever.

We make birthdays a big deal for each family member. The kids don't always get a blow-out party (four per year would blow out the checking account!), but we always make birthdays a special time for everyone. After we have the cake and open the presents, we go around the family circle and tell what we love about the birthday person. It is one of those moments of tears, laughter and love that just cannot be replaced. If we could not afford to buy a single gift, we could still do this, and walk away afterwards knowing we had all been blessed and encouraged!

4. Atmosphere

By atmosphere I refer to the overall tone of a home—the feeling we have living there day in and day out. For a family to be close, the atmosphere must be great! It is impossible for a family to be united, "tight" and together when the atmosphere is bad. What do we need to do, then, to have a great atmosphere?

The basic attitude of being positive and joyful is essential to creating a great atmosphere. We ought to have the conviction in our homes that "God is with us, life is great, and no matter what happens, we're going to come out ahead!" Life can be difficult at times. There are many setbacks and disappointments along the way for parents and kids. If we keep up our faith in God on a daily basis and stay positive, even with the "little" things, the whole family feels better, and feels closer to one another.

As the leaders of the family, parents set the tone. If we become negative, the family will pull apart. When we are gloomy and anxious, we cannot provide the spark and inspiration to pull the group together to accomplish great things.

Don't let a sour, negative child ruin the atmosphere of a home! There is nothing worse than for one whiny, complaining sourpuss to be allowed to ruin it for everyone else. No one wants to be around someone like this. Kids won't want to be at dinner with them or have family devotionals with "old gloom and doom" frowning away from the sidelines. We must turn this around if our family is to be close.

But we must take it a step higher—we must go from being positive and joyful to having fun and laughter in our home if we are to have an atmosphere conducive to closeness. We need to be able to pull the family together, kick back, and have some great times. Especially when there have been some difficulties and hardships, we just need to relax, laugh and have a great old time!

It is amazing how laughter and fun brings a family closer. If we can laugh together, then we like being together, and we like each other, and that adds up to unity! If we can laugh at each other, with each other, at ourselves, and at life, we will be close. Laughter and fun have a way of breaking down the barriers and letting us be ourselves, without pretension. It helps everyone to feel accepted, loved and at home.

In our family, we do plenty of things to get the laughter going. Sometimes at dinner we have "Joke Night." Everybody gets to tell their latest joke. Some are really lousy, but that's part of the fun. Sometimes the kids beg to hear the old jokes they have heard me tell countless times before. They love to hear stories of all the embarrassing things that have happened to me. Alexandra, our youngest, is not too good at telling jokes. She is hilarious but not when she *tries* to be. Her manner of joke telling is to yell out "Joke! Joke!" right in the middle of dinner. It always gets a laugh (I just hope she's not doing it at school!).

Consider these verses:

> A happy heart makes the face cheerful, but heartache crushes the spirit (Proverbs 15:13).

> All the days of the oppressed are wretched, but the cheerful heart has a continual feast (Proverbs 15:15).

> A cheerful look brings joy to the heart, and good news gives health to the bones (Proverbs 15:30).

> A cheerful heart is good medicine, but a crushed spirit dries up the bones (Proverbs 17:22).

We need to do whatever it takes to transform our homes into positive, fun places where laughter is heard frequently. If we do, our families will be close!

But besides the atmosphere of attitude, the physical environment needs to be pleasant—the kind of place people like to be. We need to keep our houses clean, neat and orderly. It's hard to feel great about being together when the place looks like a bomb just went off. Dirt, filth and clutter do not create an atmosphere of closeness; they actually say that we do not care enough about our family to show the respect to keep the place up. When the environment says "we don't care," then people stop caring about each other!

We need to work at making our homes attractive. When the place is bright, cheerful and inviting, it helps everyone feel good about being there. If God was concerned about the beauty and appearance of his home (the temple) then we, too, should be concerned about ours. My wife excels at doing a great deal with a little money. By spending a few dollars here and there, and by carefully and skillfully arranging the colors, furniture, etc., she can transform a house into a place in which we love to live! We do not have to become materialistic or lose our focus on God to have an attractive home. It just takes some thought and extra effort.

We recently lived in an 1,100-square-foot apartment for eight months. Yes, all six of us! It was tight, but we made it work. Geri fixed up the place as best she could. We all decided to make it a great time, and it was! It was during those months of cramped living that God blessed us by allowing us to reach out to our downstairs neighbors and bring them to Christ. The atmosphere of closeness that we create can make a tremendous difference in our lives and the lives of others.

These are just a few of the things we have done to create a great atmosphere. I would urge you to evaluate the atmosphere of your home, and if it is not what it needs to be, change it!

❦

In a world torn by division and loneliness, a warm, unified family is one of the greatest blessings we can ever enjoy. It is our prayer that you will devote yourself to making your home the place of warmth and closeness that God intends and that God will crown your efforts with success.

FINISHING

CHAPTER **11**

Sex and Dating

Do not be overcome by evil, but overcome evil with good
(Romans 12:21).

W
E LIVE IN A SEXUALLY CONFUSED WORLD. OUR CHILDREN ARE
confronted with temptations that most of us did not
have to face until we were much, much older. If there
is any realm where they need guidance, this is it!
Wherever we are today, we need to start working with our kids in
this area and the sooner, the better!

What do our children need in their hearts and characters to
overcome the sexual challenges and temptations they will face?

An assured trust in God

> "For I know the plans I have for you," declares the Lord,
> "Plans to prosper you and not to harm you, plans to give you
> a hope and a future" (Jeremiah 29:11).

Our children must believe that God is good and that whatever he says and does is for their benefit. If God forbids something, he is not just trying to punish them, and he is not being arbitrary—it is for their good.

Kids must also believe that God knows best. They must trust that God's wisdom is higher than theirs and that he not only is amazingly intelligent, but that he has the capacity to sovereignly arrange the specific events of their lives into a beautiful plan. It naturally follows that since marriage is God's will for the vast majority of people (1 Corinthians 7:1-7), then God has someone in mind for them to marry, and he will move heaven and earth to get the two of them together!

Knowing and believing these things about God prevents a sullen resignation or active rebellion against his will. Kids who have a serene, poised trust in God and his good plan for their lives don't allow their passions to lead them into sexual sin or into marrying someone outside God's kingdom. It makes them virtually unfazed by any teasing, ridicule or pressure they may receive for their "strange" high standards from their schoolmates and friends.

I remember when I was still a teenager (age 19) and Geri and I were dating, I would from time to time receive unsolicited advice from my college fraternity brothers. They could not understand why Geri and I were not together every waking (and sleeping!) hour. "Someone's going to take her away from you if you don't watch out," they would counsel. I am sure some of them thought there had to be something wrong with my sexual orientation since Geri and I were not going to bed together. Well, there wasn't and there isn't! Some of the advice was well-intentioned and some was just plain ridicule. But the fact is, after over 20 years of marriage, Geri and I still are still happily in love. I don't know where all of my friends ended up in their marriages, but I have heard about quite a few tragic break-ups that have occured. The only difference in them and me was that I did it God's way. And because of that, he poured out his blessings upon me, as he will for anyone who trusts and obeys him.

What I am saying is that we must teach our kids to trust God absolutely. They must trust in the goodness of God's *heart,* that he only wants the best for them. They must trust in the goodness of his *word,* especially as it applies to sexual matters. And finally, they must trust in the goodness of God's *ways,* that if they seek him first, he will orchestrate all the events of their lives to place them with that special someone they can love, cherish and enjoy forever!

A positive view of sex

> So God created man in his own image, in the image of God he created him; male and female he created them (Genesis 1:27).

> God saw all that he had made, and it was very good (Genesis 1:31).

Sex is a beautiful creation of God. Sexual attraction and sexual pleasure are intrinsically good. There is nothing evil about the sexual part of our nature. It is something God has placed within us to assure the propagation of the next generation and to give us joy and pleasure in life.

Some of us mistakenly believe that sex is the devil's domain and was the "forbidden fruit" of the Garden of Eden. Maybe we picked this up from weirded-out medieval theology or from the misguided, twisted understanding of holiness we got from our childhood churches, but this attitude is wrong, unhealthy and will lead our children into frustration, guilt and sexual sin.

Don't let sex be taken away from God and turned over to Satan! It is God's property! Satan has tried to take it away from God, twist it for selfish purposes and warp its original beauty. Don't let your children grow up thinking that all of the people out in the world are *really* having a great time sexually, but if someone serves God, they never will. It is a lie on both counts!

Teach them that God wants them to have a great sexual life, but at the right time, in the right way, with the right person. This knowledge takes most of the punch right out of sexual temptation. Why? Because if kids know that sex is good and that God is going to give them a great marriage with a wonderful sexual experience, then the attractiveness and appeal of the world's counterfeits lose their power! Our kids are in a battle for a godly understanding of sex. Half the battle is controlling the passions; the other half is realizing that sexual sin is falsely presented by the world.

I will never forget how this was brought home to me when Elizabeth was about six years old. She had (and still has) a vivid, active imagination. When she began to hear dirty words at school, she could not get them out of her mind. Even though she knew this was wrong, she could not seem to shake it.

One day, I asked her to tell me the words with which she was struggling. She was appalled at first, but then, in almost a whisper, she told me each one. Within reasonable limits, for someone her age, I defined them for her. She was amazed! She hadn't really known what they meant, and when she found out, she either laughed them off as ridiculous or was disgusted at their grossness. I don't think she ever had another serious problem with that kind of thing again. What had happened? By putting the filth out in the daylight, Elizabeth was able to see it for what it was, and kick it out of her mind. Exposure of the bad and the positive presentation of the good is the best possible defense against sin!

A reverence for the human body

> It is God's will that you should be sanctified; that you should avoid sexual immorality; that each of you should learn to control his own body in a way that is holy and honorable, not in passionate lust like the heathen, who do not know God; and in this matter no one should wrong his brother or take advantage of him... (1 Thessalonians 4:3-6).

We are created in the image of God. As such, our bodies are honorable, noble and worthy of our highest respect. The body is not an evil thing to be disdained, feared and ashamed of, in contrast to the spirit and soul, which are pure. The term "the flesh" (or sinful nature in the NIV) is not equated in the Scriptures with the term "the body." We are to honor God with our bodies (1 Corinthians 6:20). If our bodies are basically evil, then how can we honor God with them? "The flesh" has reference not to our literal physical being but to those rebellious impulses in us that lead us to warp our legitimate desires to selfish ends. It refers to that part of our nature that longs for independence from God and that wants no control or limitation of its will.

Kids who respect their own bodies and the bodies of others possess a great weapon against sexual sin. Why? Since they understand that sex is honorable, they are able to see through the lustful display of sex in pornography, television, music videos, movies and the like as something that degrades people and degrades sex. Young people who learn to be abhorred and offended by the flaunting of the human body are not likely to be drawn into the mire of lust and pornography.

A high regard for the body is one way to deal with the temptation of masturbation. When we teach kids that the purpose of sex is for the conception of children and for the enjoyment and fulfillment of husband and wife, they realize that masturbation falls outside the purposes of God. They see that sex is meant to be an act of unselfish love between a husband and wife. It follows then, that to seek sexual fulfillment outside of that relationship is foolish and sinful. Although the Bible does not deal with the subject of masturbation directly, it is my conviction that it is wrong, for the above reasons and more. It is virtually always associated with lust; it becomes enslaving; it creates a selfish attitude toward sex and offends the conscience, thus paralyzing a child with guilt. We should urge our children not to become involved in this unhealthy practice.

177

The teaching of an honorable respect for the body elevates the whole essence of sex to another plane. It puts your child on the high ground of righteousness, rather than in a defensive position in which he or she is always having to fight off temptation. And when you are on the high ground, you usually win the battle!

A respect for the opposite sex

> In the Lord, however, woman is not independent of man, nor is man independent of woman. For as woman came from man, so also man is born of woman. But everything comes from God (1 Corinthians 11:11-12).

Men and women are in adversarial roles more so today than ever before. The gender conflict that used to be amusing or, at most, annoying has in recent years turned downright ugly. Sexual harassment, date rape, inequitable pay scales—these are but a few of the issues that have heightened a conflict that traces its roots back to the Garden of Eden.

The solution to this problem is to teach your children to respect the opposite sex. Teach them to value the difference between the genders and not to ridicule or disdain them.

Young boys should not look down upon girls as silly, emotional, fickle weaklings. Teach your boys to respect the intelligence, talents and competence of women in all fields of endeavor and to appreciate and respect their contributions, whenever and wherever they make them.

As boys grow up, they must not view women as sex objects, placed at their disposal for the gratification of their lustful desires. Young men should be taught that they are responsible for controlling their own passions. Never let your sons buy into the worldly idea that the burden of saying "no" falls upon the girl alone and that if a girl is "easy," then she deserves to be taken advantage of.

In a like manner, girls must also be taught to respect boys. When girls are young, they must see boys as more than clumsy, insensitive, rude oafs who function at just above cave man level. As they grow older, girls need to respect boys' built-in desires to lead, to achieve, and to prove themselves in the competitive male environment. Some in the feminist movement would have us believe that men are basically lustful and exploitative and that women should be perpetually on guard against them, never giving their hearts to any man fully, in order to avoid being hurt or taken advantage of. Others of this mind-set look at men as basically unfeeling, insensitive, disloyal bums who will walk out on women at a moment's notice. We all know men who are this way and realize that there is some truth in these stereotypes. But it is wrong to allow or encourage our girls to grow up feeling this way about men—if we do, we set them up for a life of misery and conflict.

Teach mutual respect! Model it in your marriage. Then your kids will escape the warped, over-reactive ways of the world. They will have a healthy respect for the opposite gender that will lead them to a joyful marriage and to a peaceful adjustment in life.

A high view of marriage

Marriage should be honored by all... (Hebrews 13:4).

Marriage has fallen on hard times. About half of the people who get married do not stay together and many of those that do stay together are not very happy. It is no surprise then that many people do not respect marriage. Many critics are actively hostile to marriage, blaming it for our personal and social problems. They look at it as the poorest choice out of many available options to arrange the sexual and personal relationships of men and women. Even in the church, some of us have adopted these kinds of worldly, unbiblical attitudes. Perhaps we have suffered through a bad marriage (or two, or three. . .), or perhaps we have been listening to the worldly voices. Whatever the reason, some of us find it hard to wholeheartedly recommend marriage to our children.

We must formulate our convictions from the Scriptures and not by our own failures or by the persuasion of worldly thought. God himself designed marriage—and he did a great job of it! Marriage is not the problem, *people* are! When we get *us* right, marriage comes out just fine!

The influence of the world here is pervasive. If your kids took a poll in their classrooms, how many children would be from single-parent homes (either by illegitimate birth or by divorce)? Many of their classmates are now with a stepparent. Others are in situations where the man and woman are living together. Still others are from homes where the marriage is devoid of love and perhaps even filled with verbal and physical conflict. And the portrait of family life painted by television, literature and film does little to raise our sights any higher.

We must counteract this with the biblical teaching that marriage is a beautiful relationship, designed by God for the happiness of men and women and for the proper environment in which to raise children.

Our children must learn that marriage, in spite of its difficulties, is wonderful, is from God and is a glorious thing! We should let them know that the years of courtship are just that—years to let God lead them to the right person. We must teach them that the privileges of sexual intimacy and of living under the same roof are reserved *only* for people who are married in the eyes of God and according to the laws of the land. We must teach our children to look forward to their engagement and wedding days as two of the greatest days of their lives. We should model for them a noble and romantic view of marriage that they unashamedly uphold, not only for themselves, but for others.

If we deeply believe these things and teach them faithfully to our kids, they will one day fulfill in their lives the dream of a wonderful marriage.

A commitment to date and marry within the church

> Do not be yoked together with unbelievers. For what do righteousness and wickedness have in common? Or what fellowship can light have with darkness? (2 Corinthians 6:14).

> . . .she is free to marry anyone she wishes, but he must belong to the Lord (1 Corinthians 7:39).

Marriage to those outside God's kingdom always has been disapproved by God (Nehemiah 13:27) and has inevitably had disastrous consequences for God's people (1 Kings 11:1-2). It is my own solid conviction that it is wrong for a disciple of Jesus to marry someone who is not also a disciple. It is also my conviction that since dating is the means by which we select a marriage partner, then our children should date only within the family of God, the church.

This is a heart-conviction that we must give our children early in life. In some ways, it naturally attaches itself to all else we believe. I don't know how much time Geri and I have spent actually teaching this, but it has certainly never become a point of dispute between us and our kids. Why? Because they have such strong desires to be disciples themselves that they could never imagine choosing to spend the rest of their lives with someone who does not!

What do we do when our children are attracted to someone at school who is interested in them and is a reasonably nice person? We have taught our children that it is fine to be friends with kids like this, but they must not become romantically involved. We don't want our children to withdraw from others, but our kids know without question how Geri and I feel about them going out with someone like this—it is strictly off-limits.

Our daughter is presently in high school, and she sometimes gets asked out by boys at school. She gives a pleasant, routine explanation that she is appreciative of the invitation, but that she chooses to go out only with guys from her church because of her desire to be united spiritually with whomever she dates. She is careful not to make it a personal rejection, nor to come across like a self-righteous prude. She often responds by inviting them to come with her to church or to teen activities. She is entirely comfortable with this, because it is something she deeply believes as a dedicated disciple of Jesus Christ.

I would urge all of us to put these convictions deep within our children's souls! Then their hearts never will be pulled away from God because they get emotionally involved with someone outside his kingdom. If we teach this and if we lay a careful foundation of conviction beneath it, we will live to see our children marry wonderful Christians who will be a blessing not only to them, but to us as well.

An understanding of the nature of sexual temptation

> Put to death, therefore, whatever belongs to your earthly nature: sexual immorality, impurity, lust, evil desires... (Colossians 3:5).

Sexual attraction and sexual temptation are the most powerful forces your children will have to grapple with as they enter into maturity. Problems arise not only from desires within themselves but from a world that increasingly flaunts sex before children at younger and younger ages. We must provide our children with the biblical teaching and advice they will need to successfully find their way down this difficult path.

In tackling the issue of lust, we must first understand what it is and what it is not. Let us go through this step by step together.

(1) Sexual attraction is not necessarily sin. Seeing a girl or boy and thinking they are cute, beautiful or handsome is not wrong. It is quite normal. If kids equate sexual attraction to

sexual lust, they will be tormented by guilt and frustrated by the impossibility of overcoming their God-given impulses. Some kids with extremely sensitive consciences will need plenty of help here.

(2) Sexual lust occurs when your child crosses the line from attraction to arousal. More specifically, lust occurs when:
- they continue to look at something explicitly sexual.
- they look at someone for the purpose of desiring them sexually.
- they engage in fantasies involving sexual images or sexual activity.

(3) Sexual lust does *not* occur just because any of the following things happen to your child:
- their heart skips a beat when someone they like walks up.
- they notice an attractive girl or a cute boy.
- they struggle with the urge to look at a pornographic magazine or video.
- something comes before their eyes that will incite lust, but they quickly look away.
- a sexual thought passes through their minds.

(4) We must help our kids discern the difference between list number two and list number three. Some kids are so sensitive in conscience that they equate temptation with lust. Not so! We know Jesus was tempted to lust because the Bible says he was tempted in every way (Hebrews 4:15). Don't let Satan throw your children into pits of self-accusation simply because they have to fight off evil thoughts.

Other kids who have very little conscience will deceive themselves into thinking everything is fine, when it is not. Kids like this will flirt with lust and end up getting trapped by it because they are not heeding the Bible's teaching to "flee from sexual immorality" (1 Corinthians 6:18) as they should.

(5) All children need to be taught to have a sober fear of sexual lust and of sexual sin and to stay far away from them. This includes guarding their hearts (Proverbs 4:23), their eyes (Pro-

verbs 4:25) and the pathway of their feet (Proverbs 5:8). If they do fall in any way, pray to God that they tell you quickly or that you find out quickly! Sexual sin must be rapidly repented of before it has opportunity to gain a serious foothold in our children's lives.

(6) Be very careful with television and videos. Geri and I do not allow our children to watch certain channels or certain movies. If need be, cancel your cable TV service or drop the offensive channels. Even the major networks are becoming more liberal in their programming. Never let your kids just sit in front of the TV and watch whatever happens to be on the air.

(7) Help children work through any thoughts that are deviant, abnormal or weird. Some kids have active imaginations and their minds may wander into some very strange territory! If they talk to you about things like this, listen carefully. Ask enough questions to get the full picture. Whatever you do, *don't* over-react! Usually just being able to talk about it goes a long way towards solving the problem for a youngster. After you hear everything, give them any guidance they may need to clear their minds of the unwholesome thoughts.

(8) The best defense is a good offense. A mind can only think one thing at a time. Teach your kids to stop trying *not to sin* but instead to fill their minds with great thoughts (Colossians 3:1-4; Romans 8:1-17; Philippians 4:8-9). If they focus on serving God, reading their Bibles, praying and serving others, they won't have the time to be dragged into sin.

An open door to talk

...speaking the truth in love, we will in all things grow up... (Ephesians 4:15).

We have already made the point that the lines of communication must be completely open between our kids and us. In no area is it any more important than in sexual matters. As we said in

184

the last section, we should always encourage them to talk to us about sexual issues and we should listen carefully when they do.

When do we teach our kids about sex and how? I will give a few pointers here:

(1) Don't be afraid to talk about sexual things with your children at a fairly young age. Even in preschool they may hear talk from playmates or see programs on TV about which they need to ask us. Help them to know what behavior is acceptable. Teach them about the private parts of their bodies that others should not touch. Also teach them not to touch these parts on others.

(2) In the elementary school years it will be time for the old "birds and the bees" talk. It is best for Mom to talk with the girls and Dad to talk with the boys. It usually has to happen somewhere between eight and 10, depending on a child's maturity level.

I use the Bible to help. I remember having "the talk" with David when he was around 10. I started out in Genesis 1. I read about the creation of man and woman and said, "Son, what do you think it means when God tells the man and woman to be fruitful?" I was so impressed with my brilliance at using this approach that I got caught completely flat-footed by David's reply. He looked at me very excitedly and said, "Oh, that's where we have lots of conversions and the church grows real fast." Well, I appreciated my son's spiritual point of view on fruitfulness, but we were there to talk about another kind of fruitfulness!

I will not go into detail in this book on how to have "the talk" except to say that when we do we should speak positively, forthrightly and comfortably. Usually, parents are more embarrassed than the kids!

A willingness to be guided

> Listen, my son to your father's instruction and do not forsake your mother's teaching. They will be a garland to grace your head and a chain to adorn your neck (Proverbs 1:8-9).

185

Our kids need to let us guide them as they enter into the years of dating and courtship. They do not know what is best, and they need to realize this and depend on their parents to help them. Stubborn, arrogant children who think they are wise enough to run their own lives are sadly mistaken. If they do not change their attitudes and become learners, they will suffer heartbreak of immense proportions. Parents, we *must* put a learner's heart into our children, especially when it comes to sex and dating.

Let me share with you some of the practical guidance Geri and I have given our children on dating matters.

We don't mind our elementary and middle-school-age kids having special friends at church of the opposite sex. There are two requirements: They have to keep it on a casual basis, and the relationship must be spiritually encouraging. Our boys have both had girls in the church that they have "liked" and who have liked them back. They have given each other small gifts and have written letters when they were out of town and have even talked long distance occasionally on the phone. We consider this to be positive and healthy. But we do not allow them to "go steady" or say they "love" each other as some of the kids at their school do. We think they are too young for that. As our 6-year-old daughter Alexandra says, "I know, I can't get mushy yet!"

Our oldest daughter went on her first "date" in middle school. She met one of the younger boys at a church party and they (sort of!) spent the evening together there. We brought her and took her home. This is the way to start your kids dating: low key, many other people around, and no riding anywhere together without adults in the car.

As Elizabeth grew older, we began to allow her to go out on "car dates." She had to be with very responsible, trustworthy young men from church and we had to approve every aspect of the plan. We did not let her go out for a lengthy time, and she had to be in early. We had to know exactly where she was, and it had to be *at least* a double-date situation, and we had to approve the other couple(s) on the date.

We gradually have given Elizabeth more freedom as she has grown older. She has demonstrated a great attitude; she is desirous of doing the right thing and wants our guidance. That attitude, plus her responsible conduct, has earned our trust and has enabled us to give her more freedom. But even so, we still have to give our permission before she goes out, and we still feel free to give plenty of direction about the specifics of what goes on and when she gets in.

Some of us may be new to all of this, and so are our kids. If your kids are older, you need to sit down and have a talk before you start changing everything. Teach them the basics and background in the Scriptures first and then move ahead. It is more of a challenge to change the old bad habits than it is to set up great ones from the outset. But I would urge you to do all you can to make up for any lost time by giving your children the advice they so desperately need in the areas of sex and dating.

A joyful life in God's kingdom

...the joy of the Lord is your strength (Nehemiah 8:10).

A joyful, fulfilling life is one of the greatest safeguards available to protect our children from sexual sin. If their lives are full of happiness, then there is far less inclination for kids to go looking in the wrong places for fulfillment. Young people who are having fun in God's kingdom don't need or desire the bad things of the world.

Joyful lives for our children must start in our own households. How many kids have become more attracted to sin because they experienced only misery, anger and quarreling in their homes?

We simply *must* build happy families. First, we need to create unity. If there is closeness among all the brothers and sisters and if the whole family has great, joyful times together, then children will be much more likely to strive to live in such a way as to earn

187

their family's respect and approval. Second, we must model loving, warm relationships as husbands and wives. When our kids admire our marriages, they naturally will be all the more eager to imitate us and listen to our advice about sex and dating.

Our children also need to be a part of an exciting, spiritual ministry for kids in the church. They need to have friends their own ages who are godly, wholesome and sharp. Youngsters who are surrounded by peers at church whom they respect, have fun with and can talk to are much less likely to be drawn away from God to seek fulfillment and approval from worldly companions.

I urge you to pitch in and help to make the kids' ministry at your church, from the nursery to high school, the best it can be! Get behind it, get involved, get to know the teachers and the other parents. Encourage your kids to be a part of everything. Give rides, offer to host events in your home, shell out the necessary money, go the second mile—do whatever it takes to help put together a great work for the kids!

One thing I would especially encourage is the sending of our kids to the church-sponsored camps, retreats and seminars that are available around the country. In just a few short days, these special events can do more than we can possibly imagine to encourage our children to stay faithful and pure. When our kids see so many others from God's kingdom all together in one place, they realize they are part of the hottest thing going on Planet Earth! It gives a tremendous boost to their spirits and a great incentive to never compromise their sexual standards. Another benefit is that they will make some friends at these events that they can write, call, and keep up with long after it is over. If some of these new acquaintances are from the opposite gender, this will go very far toward giving our kids the hope and confidence that they will one day find and marry the most awesome person in the world!

❦

Nowhere are the troubled times in which we live more challenging than in the area of sex and dating. If we build our children's lives on the foundation of God's word, they will be protected from the pitfalls and heartache of sexual sin, and will grow up to build strong marriages and families of their own.

12

Special Life Situations

God sets the lonely in families...(Psalm 68:6).

So all the elders of Israel gathered together and came to Samuel at Ramah. They said to him, "You are old and your sons do not walk in your ways..." (1 Samuel 8:4-5).

We will now address three situations that require special attention: single-parent families, composite families and the children of leaders.

Single-Parent Families

The statistics tell the story—the number of single-parent households is skyrocketing. More and more people are having to cope with this very challenging family situation. It is difficult enough to raise children when there are two people available to handle the emotional, physical and spiritual stresses. How much more formidable to face them alone!

We now will examine several of the obstacles that single parents must confront and overcome.

Loneliness

The burdens of parenthood are heavy, and without a spouse to help share the emotional load, loneliness can become a debilitating problem. Children are wonderful companions, but they are young and dependent and cannot understand all the feelings we experience as adults. Add to this the fact that divorce or death could be the reason for singleness, and we see how the feelings of loneliness can become overwhelming. The same is true for mothers who have had children out of wedlock. Perhaps they were counting on marriage but were left by themselves to raise the child (or children) alone. The pain, anger and hurt can weigh them down with a depressing, empty feeling of despair, with little hope for change.

So it is for those without God. But for those of you who belong to him, how different life is and how different your attitude ought to be! I am reminded of a great statement about God from one of the prophets:

> "For your Maker is your husband—the Lord Almighty is his name—the Holy One of Israel is your Redeemer; he is called the God of all the earth. The Lord will call you back as if you were a wife deserted and distressed in spirit—a wife who married young, only to be rejected," says your God. "For a brief moment I abandoned you, but with deep compassion I will bring you back. In a surge of anger I hid my face from you for a moment, but with everlasting kindness I will have compassion on you," says the Lord your Redeemer (Isaiah 54:5-8).

I believe that God, in a unique sense, becomes the husband of single mothers who have committed their lives to him. The passage above indicates that God himself takes on the role of husband, since there is no man in the house. Now tell me, is there a better husband available than this one?

Whether you are a single mother or single father, God cares about you! He feels for you and will be with you in a special way to meet your needs. As he cared for the rejected Hagar and her son Ishmael (Genesis 21:17-21), he will wrap his arms of protection around you and your family. God understands loneliness—he once gave up a son. The Lord himself will comfort you through his Spirit when your prayers of anguish are beyond expression (Romans 8:26-27).

But you also have another resource—the kingdom of God, the church. God sets the lonely in families; and when you were born again to become God's child, you became a member of his great worldwide family.

I urge you, become a functional part of the church. Don't let yourself withdraw in frustration and independence. Learn to express your needs to others—they cannot help you if they do not know your needs. And many times, unless people have been there themselves, they will not fully grasp all that you feel. Don't let this become a stumbling block to you. Say what you think without a complaining spirit, and you will find yourself surrounded by people who want to help.

Another step I would urge you to take is to develop a close relationship with a spiritually strong two-parent family in your church. Find a family with an excellent mother and father who can be special friends to you, and who want to help care for your children. Encourage your kids to be close to theirs. Work to make the relationship between your families so close that you feel entirely comfortable with your children sleeping over at each other's houses. You also want these two parents to feel free to get involved with the discipline and training of your kids. These people cannot pay your bills or live your life for you, but they can lighten your load, increase your joy, and give you a wonderful sense of security.

You also must build up your own family life. Even if there are only two of you, that still qualifies as a family! Think of yourself as a family member *first* and a single person *second*. The chapters in this book entitled "Foundations of a Spiritual Family" (Chapter 9) and "A Close Family" (Chapter 10) are written for you, too. Have meals together. Start your own family traditions. Have family devotionals. Rejoice together and enjoy the family you have!

Self-pity

If you do not guard your heart carefully, the loneliness and hurt you feel can turn into self-pity. Self-pity is that feeling of "Poor me, no one understands how hard this is. No one appreciates the struggles I have, and why is this happening to me, anyway?"

Self-pity is dangerous because it seems so innocent and is so understandable. But if you let it go unchecked, it will destroy your soul. Let me ask you, who is the one person who ever lived who had the greatest excuse to feel sorry for himself? You know the answer—Jesus Christ. Did he indulge in self-pity? You know the answer again—absolutely not!

Give up clinging to the idyllic dream you had of a "white picket fence" kind of life, and stop thinking about what "might have been." Realize that everyone has problems, including married people. As great as marriages are meant to be, many of them are hell on earth. Would you change places with someone in a bad marriage? Life is not easy for *anyone*. And remember, trials and difficulties are what God uses in all our lives to make us stronger people.

As you deal with your own emotions, you must realize that your children need you to be strong. If you are too open with your tears, hurts and feelings in front of them, they will become insecure and fearful. You can let them know that you are hurting at times, but you must do so in a state of emotional self-control. Pour out your tears and anguish to God and to friends in the church. But please, guard your children from coming to believe that you are falling completely apart.

You must conquer the "I just can't do it" attitude. God says, "Yes, you can!" He also says that he will not let you go through anything that inevitably will destroy you (1 Corinthians 10:13). Whatever the challenge, be it emotional, financial or spiritual, God will be there for you. Trust in God, get to work, and you will find that there is no problem you cannot solve.

Guilt

Some of you are single parents because of sexual sin. Now, you live every day with the reminder of your rebellion. Others of you are divorced and you have to face the fact that your own weaknesses are part of the reason that the marriage did not work. The shame, guilt and sense of failure can be absolutely crushing.

Guilt feelings can cause you to be a poor parent. You may fail to discipline your kids because you are paralyzed with guilt. You feel responsible for your children being in a single-parent home and to make up for this you try to indulge their every whim. You also may find that you lash out at the children in anger and frustration, only to be seized later with bitter remorse.

I urge you to read great passages in the Bible like Psalm 38, 51 and 103, and scriptures such as Ephesians 1-3 which describe the completeness of your forgiveness in Christ. You cannot go back and change what you have done—that is why Jesus died for you! Accept God's grace; let him help you deal with the conse-quences of your sins and mistakes, and press forward to live a great life!

Being overwhelmed

You are going to have to do several things to cope with the challenges of your schedule, finances and job:

(1) Become disciplined in the use of your time. You will have precious little to waste! Plan out your days. Get your family on a regular schedule. You cannot live as if you have no children! They need regular feeding times, meal times, etc., in their schedules and so do you. Also, spread the work load around by giving the kids regular jobs around the house.

(2) Be solution-oriented. Rely on God and tough out those situations you cannot change. But if you can improve your job, schedule, transportation or finances, then do it!

(3) Get advice. Seek out wise people who can give you ideas on how to improve your employment situation and who can help you become a more marketable employee. Others can help you in setting up a budget and managing your money. Single mothers, go to married women in the church for guidance on how to be a better mother. If you are surrounded by other singles, it is critical that you find some experienced parents to help advise you on any difficult child-rearing challenges.

Discipline problems with the children

Read the chapters in this book on discipline, obedience, etc., and put them into practice. Don't let your children grow up to be spoiled, disrespectful and unruly just because they have only one parent. Be cool, calm and consistent. Be strong with your kids. God will give you the strength to raise them right! And one other note: if you live with other singles, remember, a kid can handle only one mother, and you are it! Your roommates can help, but they must not try to carry out your role as mother. (The same principle applies to single dads.)

In closing our thoughts for single parents, I want to leave you with all the encouragement I can. Have you ever realized that the great prophet Samuel was reared in a single-parent home? Have you ever thought that perhaps Timothy was primarily influenced by his mother and grandmother? Have you ever wondered at what age Joseph died, perhaps leaving Mary, Jesus and the rest of the family without a father?

Whatever the answers to these questions, we know this: God, in his sovereign love and power, is always working everything out for our good. He is doing that for you and for your family! If you trust God and never give up, he always will work out a great plan!

Composite Families

By this term, I refer to households that are composed of a mixture of people from different families. In a family like this, there is a parent who is not the biological parent of one or more of the children and there may be children from other parents as well.

These can be very difficult situations. Any time we put together people whose backgrounds, emotions and habits are rooted elsewhere, there will be crossed wires and difficult adjustments. Many of these marriages don't survive simply because the children do not adjust to the new spouse and vice versa. If there is a combination of children, there can be envy and competition among them that causes tension and that can pry parents apart.

What can you do to make a family like this work?

Build spiritual unity

> For he himself is our peace, who has made the two one and has destroyed the barrier, the dividing wall of hostility, by abolishing in his flesh the law with its commandments and regulations. His purpose was to create in himself one new man out of the two, thus making peace, and in this one body to reconcile both of them to God through the cross, by which he put to death their hostility. He came and preached peace to you who were far away and peace to those who were near. For through him we both have access to the Father by one Spirit. Consequently, you are

no longer foreigners and aliens, but fellow citizens with
God's people and members of God's household...
(Ephesians 2:14-19).

Jesus Christ is the means of building unity in a composite
family. (When you sit down and think about it, that's exactly what
his church is!) If the parents are dedicated to Jesus, and if the
children are taught to respect and honor him also, then everyone
can come together and put aside personal feelings and preferences
for the sake of Christ. It's that simple. Unity in *any* situation is
possible only through Christ! The challenges of a composite
family only highlight the need for Jesus and make it more obvious.

Composite families need to have a very strong regularity and
focus in their family devotionals. Singing, praying, studying the
Bible together—all of these things do so much to draw everyone
close beneath the fatherly love of God. I also would suggest that
such families, especially those with older children, have weekly
open family meetings to air out feelings. The rule is this: anybody
can say anything on his or her mind, as long as he or she expresses
it respectfully. This kind of meeting will go a long way toward
forging a wonderful unity in your home!

Parents must be unified

When you married each other, your commitment was, and
still is, to be united for life. You must therefore live that way and
hammer out unity with your new spouse on every issue that could
possibly divide you.

A composite family is formed after our habits and life
patterns are set. You already have a way of going about things, and
habits don't change easily! They are reinforced by memories of
the way things used to be—memories that we cling to either out
of love or out of a desire for stability.

Parents, you will have to be the examples of the "give and
take" that will be necessary. You will have to have many talks to

197

work things out, and a great spirit of love and compromise will have to rule in your hearts.

Work out how the children will be disciplined. The new parents are going to have to be respected and to have some authority. It may not be exactly the same as if they were the biological parent, but they must have a role of leadership. If the "real" parent is protective and possessive, the new parent will have a hard time being accepted. Geri and I worked with one situation in which there was a rebellious son who was was selfish and obstinate and gave his mother extreme difficulty. After her marriage, when he would behave rebelliously, the new husband would try to step in. Even though the mother was being horribly treated by the son, she would immediately rush to his defense and undercut her husband's efforts. Although we tried to get the husband and wife to unite to help the young man, they never really listened. The family fell apart, and the husband and wife eventually divorced.

Don't let this happen to you! Work hard to hammer out unity. Talk through your differences in child rearing. Get competent, godly people to help you come up with wise solutions to any thorny problems, and you will create a harmonious family.

Win the hearts of the children

If you are the new spouse stepping into an existing family, you have your work cut out for you. You need to prepare yourself to give plenty of love and you must be very patient. You are not only marrying a spouse, you are adopting a family! They come as one package; therefore you must love and care for the children.

If the children are young or if they have never had a parent, it can make your job easier. But if the children are older and if the parent was taken away by death or divorce, you must realize that it will require immense amounts of love, understanding and prayer for you to work out a relationship. They are immature and are being tossed by currents of emotion that neither they nor you entirely understand. Love them, give them time, and pray for God to move.

If you are a man coming into a family that has older children, you need to be very patient. You must realize that you cannot step in and immediately be the heavy-handed disciplinarian. You probably will see many behavior problems that need a father's firmness, but you must proceed slowly. Give the children time to know and love you before you take on that role. And understand, with some of the older kids, you never will be able to treat them as if you had raised them from infancy.

You cannot force your way into their hearts. They will have to open the door and let you in. Some of you try to kick the door down. Others bang on the door, waiting impatiently for it to open. Others of you are angry that there is a door there at all and waste your time wishing it would go away. And finally, there are those of you who sit out on the front steps, depressed, weeping and feeling sorry for yourself because you aren't being treated better.

I would urge you to imitate God in his way of winning hearts. When we rejected him, God did not stop loving us. Instead, he loved us sacrificially and gave us his son—his very best. He patiently waited for our response and never gave up, always hoping that one day we would come to trust in his love and completely give him our hearts. If God has been so loving and patient with us, can we not do the same for our newly acquired family?

I am not saying that you should become a doormat or that you should allow yourself to be disrespected or disdained. No! If you behave as if you are not worthy of respect, you will not be respected. I am simply appealing for a loving dedication to building a relationship with the children of your new spouse.

You must not try to replace the individual they have lost. In a strange way, even if the children love you, they may be reluctant to give you their hearts because they then feel disloyal to their lost parent. The ties of children to their parents run deep. Even if the children have been terribly abused by the now-absent parents, they still have an almost mystical attachment to them. Do not try

199

to destroy that love. Give them your own love and gradually they can learn to love you both.

Children of Leaders

> He must manage his own family well and see that his children obey him with proper respect. (If anyone does not know how to manage his own family, how can he take care of God's church?) (1 Timothy 3:4-5).

> ...a man whose children believe and are not open to the charge of being wild and disobedient (Titus 1:6).

The true test of our leadership is how we lead at home. This is where God squarely places the matter, and so should we. A man cannot serve as an elder in God's church unless he has earned the respect of his wife and children and they willingly follow his footsteps down the pathway of commitment to Christ. Our families know us the best. If we fail to effectively influence those who live under our roofs, how can we lead the masses?

The Bible tells the truth about its leaders. Some were wonderful examples in family leadership, but others failed. Their stories are given to us that we might imitate the good qualities of our spiritual forbears and avoid their horrible mistakes. In the books of 1 and 2 Samuel, we have the stories of the families of Eli, Saul, David and of Samuel himself. Read these accounts, and learn from them.

I would shudder to think that one day people would say to me, after a lifetime of sacrificial service to God, what they said to Samuel: "You are old and your sons do not walk in your ways. . ." (1 Samuel 8:5). Such a statement would reflect a failure of my leadership and would leave a hollow core in all that I had tried to accomplish. As a leader I live in sober and reverent fear that, unless I am careful, my children also could be lost to God's kingdom.

I will share with you briefly six challenges that leaders and their families must face and overcome.

The pressure of a hurried schedule

Leaders need to re-read Chapters 9 and 10 and ask ourselves if our family lives have any pattern and rhythm to them at all. If they do not, we need to take steps to change this—and keep it changed. The problem with being leaders is that our work is never fully done. Can we ever say that with one more talk, one more Bible study or one more meeting we could have gotten *everything* done? I go to bed every night knowing there is an infinite amount of work left undone. If we never slept, ate or saw our families again, would we then be able to meet *all* the needs that we see around us?

We must carve out time for our families. We need to pull them aside on a regular basis, meet their needs, and bond their hearts together. If Jesus took his "family," his disciples, aside for rest and time alone (Mark 6:31), should not we?

The pressures of anxiety and concern

Leaders carry heavy loads of care, and the deeper our love and dedication, the heavier the load can be. Listen to the words of Paul:

> Besides everything else, I face daily the pressure of my concern for all the churches. Who is weak, and I do not feel weak? Who is led into sin, and I do not inwardly burn? (2 Corinthians 11:28-29).

Our children can begin to feel that there is *never* a time when we can forget about "the church" and just completely focus our attention upon them.

We must learn to cast our anxieties on the Lord (1 Peter 5:7) and leave them there! If we are always burdened, anxious,

201

distracted and preoccupied around our children, they will grow to resent us and our work. They could even come to the point that they blame God and the church for taking us away from them.

The pressure to perform and conform

Leaders' kids know that they should be exemplary. They can feel such a pressure to fulfill everyone's expectations that they lose a sense of wanting to please God. This can produce shallowness and create actors and actresses rather than genuinely spiritual children. It can also produce deceit. Leaders' kids struggle with sin and temptation (just like other kids) but sometimes cover it up because they want to protect their parents' reputations.

Our role is key to overcoming the problem. Geri and I take care to work with our children on the heart level. We want to know not just what our kids are *doing* but what they are *thinking* and *feeling*. That is what we must disciple above all—the heart! If our children's hearts are right, performance will be there and it will be solid, genuine and real because it is nurtured by deep spiritual roots.

They see the best, but also the worst, in God's kingdom

One of the great blessings of being leaders' kids is that they see firsthand the incredible power of God and get to personally meet so many of the great people he uses. My own kids have attended many awesome events, and they are friends of many of the heroes and heroines of God's kingdom.

But they also see and hear the worst. And sometimes, we don't realize how much they are hearing and how negatively it can affect them. Even recently, it came out that one of our childrens' spiritual heroes was not living the righteous life that he had claimed. I had to walk them through it and help them to focus on God so they would not become disillusioned.

Our kids also may overhear us when we express our criticisms and frustrations. They see us getting upset with something or someone in the church, and it can take their trust and joy away. They may also find out that we ourselves have our critics and opponents. They can begin to resent these people and develop a sour attitude about how "unfairly" we are being treated. We hopefully can get over our anger at something like this, but the kids may not! My advice? Use great discretion in your speech— little eyes are watching, little ears are hearing. If we are not careful, we will destroy their idealism and their love for God's people.

Pride and self-righteousness

As public leaders, we attain somewhat of a celebrity status. Even though we tell them that "we are only human like you," (Acts 14:15), people are going to treat us with deference. Hopefully, this does not go to our heads. But, if we are not careful, it may go to our children's heads!

They can begin to form their whole identity around being the child of a leader. They begin to think they are better than other kids in the church. They hang back and wait for the other kids to initiate with them because they look at themselves as set apart. Church members are always coming up to them saying "Oh, aren't you so and so's son (or daughter)? Aren't you cute! I've heard all about your parents. They tell so many great stories about you!" You can be sure that this has its effect on our youngsters' little egos!

Through the years, Geri and I have tried to guard our kids from being treated differently from the other kids in church. We have encouraged their relationships with other members' children and have challenged our kids whenever we have seen any appearance of snobbishness. If they have any leadership among the other kids at church, they are going to have to earn it by their examples and not be given it just because of who their parents are.

Pressure from parents on the kids to be leaders and high achievers

> It was he who gave some to be apostles, some to be prophets, some to be evangelists, and some to be pastors and teachers,...(Ephesians 4:11).

> Are all apostles? Are all prophets? Are all teachers? Do all work miracles? (1 Corinthians 12:29)

> To one he gave five talents of money, to another two talents, and to another one talent, each according to his ability...(Matthew 25:15).

> "If anyone would come after me, he must deny himself and take up his cross and follow me" (Matthew 16:24).

Now this is a sensitive area! Using these scriptures as a starting point, let's try to draw some clear, logical conclusions:

- Everyone is called to be a disciple.
- Not everyone is called to be a public leader.
- Leadership talent is a gift from God.
- People have different amounts of talent and are thus granted different amounts of responsibility.
- If we do not exercise our talents, whatever they are or however many we have, we are in disobedience to God.
- The degree of our talent in any area has nothing to do with our inherent value before God, since he is the one who gave it to us.

Have you faced the fact that God is the one who is going to decide what your child's role in life will be? Many of us are absolutely determined to make our kids leaders and feel that somehow we have failed if they do not follow in our footsteps to become church leaders at some level. Don't we see that we are preempting God's sovereignty when we have this attitude? How prideful, and how faithless! God decides the role everyone should have, including the roles of leaders' children.

What if God has ordained our son or daughter to be someone who serves behind the scenes? Does this mean we have failed? Did God make a mistake?

Certainly moms and dads who are leaders will have an inspiring effect, and they are more likely to produce and develop leadership qualities in their kids. But the fact is, God may have given us a great kid who will never be a high-profile leader, and we are going to have to learn to accept this and be thankful about it. If we don't, we will give our child an unnecessary burden to carry.

This is true, not only of leadership, but of achievement in general. It is wrong for us to even subtly devalue one of our children because they are not super high achievers. I am afraid that some of us, in our eagerness to raise productive, achieving children, are forgetting to teach them to be righteous, sincere disciples. We are focusing on the fruit and not the root. If we do not change this, we are headed for disaster. God expected the two- talent man to produce two talents more, not five (Matthew 25). God adjusted his expectation to be appropriate to the servant's ability. And when the time came for the servant's evaluation, his commendation was equal to that of the five-talent man.

This is not to say that the children of leaders don't need to be challenged to do their best, to give their all, and to become leaders themselves. If our kids are lazy or are just holding back, they need to be called upon to do more. Some children who are highly talented are failing to put their strengths to work for God. If they do not give their talents (including their leadership skills) to the Lord, they will end up giving them to the world. Such children need to see that the greatest use of their lives and their abilities is in serving God faithfully as leaders of his people.

God is going to use our children to do all kinds of things. Let God reveal that in his own time and in his own way. Who knows, perhaps our children will rise up and do more than we ever dreamed of doing ourselves! Whatever happens, let God be God, and to him be the glory!

❦

I know there is much more to say in these three areas than I have been able to cover in a few pages. I certainly hope that the thoughts in this chapter help you in some way if you find yourself in any of these unique situations.

In the next chapter, we turn to the most important thing that any of us could hope for our children—that they become disciples of Jesus Christ.

CHAPTER **13**

Conversion

"Why were you searching for me?" he asked. "Didn't you know I had to be in my Father's house?"
(Luke 2:49).

I N ONE SENSE, THE CONVERSIONS OF YOUNG PEOPLE ARE THE
same as those who are older. They read the same Bible,
repent of the same sins, believe in the same God, and
follow the same Lord. But what at first glance seems a
simple matter is complicated by the very issue of youth. How
much can they understand? How much do they have to understand? When are they old enough? How much of the world must
they experience beforehand? How can we be sure they are making
their decisions for the right reasons? Who should be involved in
helping them? All these questions, and others like them, mean
that we need to look at this subject in greater detail.

Making the decision

Then he called the crowd to him along with his disciples
and said: "If anyone would come after me, he must deny

himself and take up his cross and follow me. For whoever wants to save his life will lose it, but whoever loses his life for me and for the gospel will save it. What good is it for a man to gain the whole world, yet forfeit his soul? Or what can a man give in exchange for his soul? If anyone is ashamed of me and my words in this adulterous and sinful generation, the Son of Man will be ashamed of him when he comes in his Father's glory with the holy angels" (Mark 8:34-38).

In the passage above Jesus sets forth the basic elements involved in the decision to become his disciple. We will discuss the critical points and apply them to teens.

(1) A deep desire. The word translated "would" (v.34) is actually the word "wishes" or "desires." Thus, the key phrase can be expressed, "If anyone desires to come after me." It follows that in order to have a valid conversion experience, young people must have a sincere desire to follow Christ that arises from within their own hearts.

(2) A denial of self. The requirement of Jesus is absolute— "he must deny himself" (v. 34). Fundamental to the idea of conversion is the concept of self-denial. The self is defined simply as who one is in the inner person, the real "me."

Unless teens see themselves for who they are apart from God, they cannot be converted. How can they deny themselves if they have never faced themselves? Young people must see how they have expressed their rebellion against God and where they will end up apart from his controlling influence.

Once they have seen this, they can decide, as do all others who follow Jesus, that they will "no longer live for themselves but for him who died for them" (2 Corinthians 5:15).

(3) **A crucified life.** Jesus challenges every follower to "take up his cross" (v. 34). What does this mean? In short, it indicates that we must die to ourselves (Galatians 2:20), to the world (Galatians 6:14) and to sin (Colossians 3:5-11). We discussed the concept of dying to ourselves in the previous section. What about the other two things to which we must die, "the world" and "sin"?

"The world" has reference to the entire system of people and powers who are not yielded to God (1 John 2:15-17, Ephesians 2:1-3). Teens considering the call to discipleship must take a hard look at the world and what it stands for before they can make a real decision. They do not have to go out and experience everything the world has to offer, but they must see in general terms what the world outside the confines of their family and teen group at church is all about.

"Sin" is much easier to deal with, since there are such clear definitions and descriptions of it in the Bible. Young people must see the sins they have committed in action, in attitude and by omission. There must be a realization that these offenses have angered and hurt God, and therefore that they must be decisively forsaken. And when sin later reasserts itself in the form of temptation, it must be crucified once again (Luke 9:23).

(4) **A committed life.** Jesus calls for his disciples to follow him (v. 34). This is the essence of discipleship—an absolute commitment to follow, obey and become like Christ. Young people must realize that this is the greatest decision they will ever make and that it is for life. Above all, they must focus on *to whom* they are making this commitment, and *for whom* they are making it—Jesus Christ! When they see the seriousness of the calling, combined with greatness of the one who calls, they are equipped to make a proper decision.

(5) **A proclaiming life.** Jesus says that we cannot be ashamed of his words (v. 38). When he called his original disciples, be bade them to become "fishers of men" (Mark 1:17). To become a

disciple, then, teens must understand and accept the commission to personally "go and make disciples" (Matthew 28:18-20). The acceptance of this challenge and the desire to give away the good news must be firmly fixed in the heart of all young people who would follow Jesus. Teens must also prepare themselves for any opposition, criticism or persecution they may receive as a result of sharing their faith.

Maturity

The question arises, "How can we know if our children are mature enough to make this decision?" Let me help by asking several questions of my own. (Note that they correspond with the section immediately previous to this one.)

(1) Are your children mature enough to make a decision about the general direction their lives will take?

(2) Do they understand who they are and who they will become apart from God? Are they ready to deny the rule of self in their lives?

(3) Have they faced up to the sins they have committed? Are they ready to crucify the sins that will continue to tempt them after they become disciples? Have they yet had to confront sexual temptation?

(4) Are they ready to follow Jesus? Do they love and admire him? Do they understand the seriousness and totality of the decision?

(5) Are they ready to share their faith? Do they see that they will receive opposition and persecution and that they will be disliked by some people?

These questions are not intended to be a checklist that we scan, looking for the "right" answers. Instead, they are meant to help us to gauge our children's capacities to think in more mature terms. Kids do not have to be adults before they can be converted to Christ. They must, however, have progressed beyond the stage of innocent childhood and be able to wrestle with the serious issues of life.

Teens cannot know exactly how the details of discipleship will work for them (and neither can we!). But what they must grasp and have the maturity to understand are the basic parameters of the decisions they are making. Then, when specific challenges arise, they will be prepared and will remain faithful.

Motivation

Motivations for any of us can become confused and clouded. The Bible teaches that our hearts are deceitful (Jeremiah 17:9) and that we cannot always accurately judge our own selves (1 Corinthians 4:3-4). If this is difficult for adults, how much more difficult will it be for inexperienced and unseasoned youth!

Here are some unworthy motivations that can creep into a young person's heart as they consider making a decision to follow Jesus:

- A desire to please their parents
- A hunger to be accepted in the church teen group
- It is the "expected" thing to do at a certain age
- The quest to be rid of a guilty conscience in order to "feel better" about real or imagined wrongdoings
- To avoid going to hell

We can see that these motives all have some good in them and that they all will be present to some degree in our children's hearts. But it is also true that this list of motives falls far short of what the Lord would expect or require of true disciples.

Here are the motives Jesus wants:

- Love for God above any other love in life
- Sincere faith in God and in Jesus Christ as God's son
- Deep convictions about God's word
- Appreciation for, and dependence upon, God's grace
- The cross of Christ—appreciation for his sacrifice
- A passionate desire to follow, serve and imitate Jesus
- An intense awareness of the need for forgiveness of sin
- A realization of lostness apart from Christ
- A determination to make a difference for God in the world

We must help our kids sort through their motivations. Some teens have an accurate picture of themselves and have hearts that are easily understood and simply motivated. Other teens are not so simple and need plenty of counsel in figuring themselves out.

Some kids may be oblivious to the fact that their motives are not deep enough or are wrongly based. If so, then we must use the Scriptures and to guide them to self-awareness. In doing this, let me caution you against making young people become so intro-spective that they begin to completely doubt themselves. We can get them so knotted up inside that they don't know which end is up anymore!

Other kids are more hard-hearted and calloused. They can take, and will need, stronger challenges to their sincerity. Don't be naive. If we fail to see through their masks and deceptions, they never will come to grips with their sin, and they never will be truly converted.

Above all, pray for wisdom and seek advice. Parents, we need plenty of help in being objective on these touchy, difficult judgment calls.

Method

How do we proceed? Who should be involved in helping our children become disciples? What is our role in the process? How much should we be involved?

Precise answers to these questions elude us, because there are simply too many variables involved. The variables include: First, the status of our current relationships with our kids—are they close or strained? Second, do our children find it easy or difficult to be open with us? Third, what is the level of our own experience, wisdom and insight in working with people in general? Fourth, are there any family conflicts that will have to be worked through during our children's conversion processes, and might we need outside help to resolve them? These are just a few of the factors that need to be considered as our children near the time of their study to become disciples.

The best approach is to look at our children's conversions as a team effort. Our parental insight and influence is absolutely essential. We must not take a passive, detached role. But the involvement of others is critical also. As parents we may not be objective in assessing our children's spiritual condition. We may be too hard or too soft, overly suspicious or completely naive. Involving a team of people assures that our children get the benefit of the best counsel and help we can provide them during this all-important time.

The other key people are our kids' friends who are already disciples. Having someone their own ages to open up with makes all the difference in the world! As peers, these young friends can better understand our kids' feelings, needs and struggles. They also serve as role models. Nothing replaces these fellow teens who serve as "best friends" and as living proof that it can be done!

I have seen my daughter Elizabeth play this crucial role in the lives of two of her friends. One was a girl she helped lead to Christ when we lived in New Jersey. This young teenager was studying the Bible with some of the women in the church. Elizabeth got involved in the studies and became her best friend. I still remember all the long talks the two of them had to help Elizabeth's friend work through all that she was being taught. The second situation occurred with another one of her New Jersey pals shortly after we moved away. He began to study to become a disciple, but became prideful and stubborn and backed away. After a visit, Elizabeth was deeply disturbed at what she saw happening to him. She got him on the phone and laid out what he was doing wrong and where he was going to end up if he did not change. By the end of the phone conversation, he was shedding tears of repentance and soon afterwards made his decision to become a disciple. Such is the power of teen friendship!

Means of understanding

In bringing our kids to conviction about their sins, we must employ great wisdom. I urge the careful study of Luke 15:11-31, commonly known as the parable of the prodigal son. This simple story of Jesus is brilliant in its grasp of human nature and will prove invaluable to us as we seek to understand the differences in our children.

Presented in the parable are the stories of two sons, a younger one who left home and an older one who remained with his father. The younger son was self-assertive and independent and outwardly rebelled against his father's will. He left home to indulge himself in the wild life of wine, women and song. The older brother, while never openly defying his father's authority, had his own set of very serious problems. He was unhappy, unforgiving, ungrateful and resentful of his duties. He seethed with underlying anger and felt mistreated and shortchanged by his father. Although he lived in close proximity to his dad, he was far from him in heart and character.

What kinds of kids do we have living in our homes? I am sure that we can see in these two boys a reflection of the different attitudes of our own children.

We cannot be permissive with our rebellious, arrogant "younger-brother" children. They are so stubborn that the only way they can learn is to come to the end of their ropes. If we bail them out of all of their "pigpens," we short-circuit the humbling process that brings them to their senses.

Our "older-brother" kids require a different approach. If we try to treat them as if they are sexually loose or on the verge of becoming drug dealers, we are making a very serious mistake. It only frustrates children like this when they feel they must uncover some dramatic sin in order to be converted. They are not "loud" sinners, they are "quiet," boring sinners! But let me assure you, their sins are just as serious as those of their rebellious younger brothers! In one sense, we even should be more wary here, because of the way the story ends. It concludes with a restored younger son but with a stubborn, impenitent older son still arguing with his father on the back steps!

In the case of my daughter Elizabeth, she became sidetracked during her conversion process in just the manner I am describing. She studied Galatians 5:19-21 and vainly searched her life for sins like sexual immorality, drunkenness, etc. What she failed to see was that her sins were primarily those of attitude—sins like pride, independence and envy. She became so frustrated and weirded-out that she actually stopped studying for a period of time.

Several months later, she began to seek a relationship with God once again. I had a very strong heart-to-heart talk with Elizabeth in which I told her that her greatest problems were her pride and her independence in her relationship with God and with other people. I reminded her of a remark she made to her mother on one occasion, "Maybe I can have a good life and accomplish great things without God." I explained to her exactly how wrong this attitude was and how it would, in the end, destroy her. I had to be very strong and very forthright. I am sure it was the most revealing conversation Elizabeth ever had in her life! She was humbled and sobered. She became deeply grieved over the way she had treated God after all that he had given to her. She quickly repented and was baptized into Christ shortly afterwards.

Many prayers

What better way to close our thoughts on conversion than this? We should pray for our children daily. Beyond all of the wisdom, expertise, methods and words, God must move! Before my children were born (or conceived!), I prayed that they would one day give their lives to Jesus. I still pray for them now, and I will continue to do so until I die. Their names will always be held up in my prayers before the throne of God wherever they are and whatever their spiritual condition. I am convinced that prayer, more than anything else, is the greatest work that I, or any parent, can do on our children's behalf.

Epilogue

It is our desire that this book lighten your load, not make it heavier. In that spirit we want to help you know how to respond, and how not to respond, to what we have taught.

We leave you with some pointers that can help you get started and stay on track.

Begin where you are. It is not too late to start. Even if your children are older, you can still make a big difference in their lives. Do not be discouraged because you have made mistakes, even of the worst sort. Do not waste time wishing you could do it all over. Courageously face your failures, learn from them, and move forward to better things. The God we serve is a God of forgiveness and recovery.

Start with the basics. Chapter One ("First Things First") and Chapter Nine ("Foundations of a Spiritual Family") form the platform upon which the rest of the teachings of this book is built. Begin there, and add the rest as you gain spiritual strength.

Get help. God has given you the church with its fellowship and guidance as the primary means of down-to-earth help. Life is too complicated for pat answers. There is no way a book can replace the tailor-made advice of wise, spiritual people. You cannot do it by yourself—you must have the help that discipling alone can provide!

Do not give up. In trying to implement the principles and teachings in this book, you may find that you and your family members do not change as quickly or as completely as you would like. Nowhere are weaknesses more exposed than in family relationships! You did not get where you are overnight, and you will not overcome everything overnight! Keep a high ideal, but measure progress by how far you have come from your starting-point.

Allow God to move and work. God is sovereignly arranging the events of your life to train and discipline you and your family. Given time, he will turn even the greatest of difficulties into a blessing. Pray, work, and wait on God to do what only he can do!

We have told you the story of the neighbors from our apartment complex that our family helped lead to Christ. They were far from God when we met, but in a few short months they have radically changed. Geri and I often consider how far this family has come and shake our heads in wonder at the great power of God. There have been some setbacks and a few difficult moments along the way, but this couple has persisted in their faith. Just a few days before the writing of these lines, their oldest son became a disciple! The younger son has now requested that someone study the Scriptures with him to help him forward on his spiritual journey.

It is examples like this that inspire us to encourage you, wherever you are, and whatever you must face:

> Don't be afraid... Remember the Lord, who is great and awesome, and fight for your brothers, your sons and your daughters, your wives and your homes (Nehemiah 4:14).

Discipleship Publications International invites you to share with us your response to this book. We want to know what is most helpful to you and what other materials you would find useful.

Write to:
Discipleship Publications International
Attn: Managing Editor
One Merrill Street
Woburn, MA 01801
U.S.A.

Fax to:
1-617-937-3889

Or call toll free:
1-800-727-8273
for current e-mail address.

Other Books Available from DPI

She Shall Be Called Woman, Volume 1
Old Testament Women
Edited by Sheila Jones and Linda Brumley

She Shall Be Called Woman, Volume 2
New Testament Women
Edited by Sheila Jones and Linda Brumley

Raising Awesome Kids in Troubled Times
By Sam and Geri Laing

Mind Change: The Overcomer's Handbook
By Thomas A. Jones

The Victory of Surrender
By Gordon Ferguson

The Disciple's Wedding
By Nancy Orr

Life to the Full
By Douglas Jacoby

For more information
on these books and many others call
1-800-727-8273

Or from outside the US call
1-617-938-7396